The Science and Techniques of Judging Dogs

Robert J. Berndt

THE SCIENCE AND TECHNIQUES OF JUDGING DOGS

ISBN 1-57779-011-1

Cataloging-in-Publication Data

Berndt, Robert J.
The science and techniques of judging dogs / Robert J. Berndt. — 1st ed.
p. cm.
ISBN 1-57779-011-1
1. Dogs--Standards. 2.Dogs--Judging. I. Title.

SF 425.2.B47 2001
636.7'0811--dc21 00-067576

This book is available at special quantity discounts for breeders and clubs for promotions, premiums, or educational use. Write for details.

Cover and Interior Design: Dianne Nelson, Shadow Canyon Graphics

First Edition
1st printing April 2001

1 2 3 4 5 6 7 8 9 0

Printed in the United States of America

Contents

The author would like to give special thanks to
Mrs. Dorothy Welsh and Mrs. Helen Lee James,
who have made numerous suggestions
about the project and the general overall plan.

A special thanks to Mrs. Fran Ippensen,
who has read the entire manuscript and
has made additional suggestions
for improvement.

Introduction

The Science and Techniques of Judging Dogs is a manual designed to help new judges as they start on their career of judging dog shows. It could also serve as a refresher course for experienced judges. It brings together in one volume the various fields of information that the judge is expected to have mastered before he enters the ring. These areas include the history of the dog, anatomy and kinesiology, movement, breed type, the role of the American Kennel Club, the actual judging in the ring, and judging evaluation.

The book takes the reader through the process in a logical, step-by-step approach from advanced breed preparation to the application for judging privileges to judging a class and the follow-through activities. It discusses the mechanics of assignments and contracts and travel.

Included in the appendix is a comparative study of several oriental breeds that could serve as a pattern for additional studies of other breeds that are similar. There is also a glossary of commonly used terms.

Available in an accompanying *Handbook of Breed Standard Analysis* is a short history of each breed along with a show photograph of a top winning specimen of the breed and an analysis in tree-chart pattern of each standard that can be used for quick reference for any point of the dog.

The material contained in this book was gathered during the author's thirty years as a dog show judge. The suggestions of other judges and breeders have been blended into the material along with library-researched information.

R.J.B.

History of the Dog

The study of the origin of the dog has interested many scholars throughout the years. They have devoted years of research to this field, arriving at various conclusions as to the exact origin of the dog. Investigation into areas of study that predate written history are always very difficult since there is so little physical evidence to either prove or disprove any particular theory. The physical evidence that does exist in the case of the dog is in two forms. The one form is the skeletal remains of dog-like ancestors found in various geographical areas around the world. The second piece of evidence involves prehistoric cave paintings also widely dispersed around the world.

Using these two pieces of physical evidence combined with the anatomical study of the present-day domestic dog, most researchers have reached the conclusion that the dog is a descendant of the wolf. Charles Darwin, the author of *On the Origin of Species,* did not believe that the wolf was the original ancestor of the dog. A number of researchers gradually began to dispute the findings of Darwin and stated that the wolf was most certainly the primary ancestor of the modern dog, but, perhaps, not the only ancestor. Evidence from the last hundred years appears now to disprove Darwin's theory relating to the dog.

The wolf or *canis lupus* existed on earth some half million years ago. Because of the small numbers and the geographical spread of the animal around the world, subspecies began to appear. In time these species locked into genetic differences and thus established the four distinct types of the wolf.

The *canis lupus* is commonly referred to as the northern grey wolf. The *canis lupus pallipes* is called the pale-footed Asian wolf. The *canis lupus arabs* refers to the small desert wolf of ancient Arabia. The *canis lupus chanco* or *laniger* describes the woolly-coated wolf that was found in the Himalayan mountains extending from Tibet through northern India.

Even though these four categories of wolves lived in somewhat limited geographical areas, there were border areas in between the main living areas of each category. In these border areas there was certain cross-breeding which resulted in additional subspecies. This would be especially

The Golden Jackal, a native of central America.

The Maned Wolf, *chrysocyon brachyurus.*

true in that region where the northern wolf, the Asian wolf, and the Tibetan wolf hunted in common. This would have resulted in a mixing of the bloods of these various groups.

Additional sub-groups can be found in the timber wolf of northern North America which produced the ancestors of the dogs that the Eskimos and the Indians of that area raised. Another wolf found on the same continent would be the prairie wolf which became the American coyote.

Some scholars believe that animals other than the wolf have figured into the development of the dog. While the wolf was the principal ancestor, they feel that in certain breeds of dog there are traces of both the fox and the jackal. Others believe that the jackal is merely another form of wolf. Genetic variability would be the result of crossbreeding of the wolf with the jackal.

Evidence used by researchers for the role of the wolf in the development of the dog includes the strong territorial instinct of the wolf. To indicate territorial limitations both the dog and the wolf use a system of scent marking with urine. The social organization of the wolf is reflected in the dog as is the hierarchical structure of the pack. Both have the alpha and beta system of animal domination. They both have a system of communication that reflects the needs of the pack.

There are similarities of physical characteristics between the wolf and the dog. These include the pattern of dentition, although the teeth of the wolf are heavier than those of the domestic dog of today. This is undoubtedly a reflection of the fact that the wolf is still a hunter today while the dog no longer has this particular need.

Toes and nails are the same between the two groups as are their eating preferences. Both prefer meat, but will eat vegetables and fruit if necessity so demands. Both the dog and the wolf have the habit of spinning around in the process of bed making. An additional similarity is the gestation period. It is sixty-three days for both.

The wolf has natural herding instincts. He used this ability to first herd and then separate certain animals from a herd he was stalking. This is the way he obtained his food. This particular quality would have been of special interest to early man who needed help in obtaining meat. Early wolf-like specimens were domesticated and selectively bred to help northern tribes control their reindeer herds.

There is evidence that these early dog breeders would tie out bitches in season so that wild wolves would breed to them in the hopes of bringing back certain of the qualities that the early domestic dogs were losing. Early dogs were kept for economic reasons and not for emotional reasons since they were working members of the clan and not household pets.

CANIS

The word *canis* refers to the family of the dog. This term is used to include the wolf, the jackal, the coyote, the fox, and the domestic dog. The word *canidae* is used to refer to the primitive ancestor of the dog. This would be the wolf-fox-like ancestor which was a predator. The canidae could be found in all parts of the world living in very different temperature zones. This forced the animal to adapt to these varying demands and resulted in the different types we see today.

The scavenger dog would undoubtedly have been one of the first semi-domesticated specimens. When man established semi-permanent housing, he began to accumulate things as he no longer had to carry them around on his back. With the establishment of permanent settlements he began to accumulate garbage. As the garbage accumulated animals began to gather to feast upon man's leftovers. Since these scavengers were beneficial to man, he tolerated them and thus acquired his first domestic dogs. Even though these dogs were semi-wild, they continued to stay around the settlements since it made finding food a less arduous task.

The feral dog is one that was domesticated at one time but at a later date returned to a wild state. This would have been a frequent phenomenon during the early period of domestication of the dog.

The pariah is a wild dog that has never been domesticated. Examples of these dogs still exist today in isolated places in the world. They continue to live in packs as did the first dogs. Such dogs are occasionally found today in the Mid-East, in Asia, and in Australia. Most of these are dingo-like dogs resembling the pale-footed Asian wolf. They retain the primitive characteristics of their ancestors.

The Arctic Gray Fox, a native of North America.

The Bat-Eared Fox, a native of central Africa.

THE NORTHERN GROUP

The *canis lupus* or the northern-type of wolf would have served as the ancestor for such breeds as the Husky, the Elkhound, the Collie, the Corgi, the Schipperke, and the Terriers. The term *canis familiaris palustris* refers to the small Spitz-like dogs.

As early as 3500 B.C. large German Shepherd and Collie type dogs could be found in central Europe while smaller Maltese-Pomeranian type dogs could be found in southern Europe.

Dogs belonging to the northern group are divided into four categories. They are:

1) Sled dogs
2) Hunting dogs
3) Sheepdogs
4) Small or Toy dogs.

Another division of this group is made on the length of the muzzle. The dog with the long muzzle and little or no stop is represented by breeds like the Collie. Dogs with a shorter muzzle and a decided stop are like the Siberian Husky.

Terriers are represented by this group. They are believed to have descended from the Spitz-Schipperke type of ancestor. They became earth dogs used for hunting to ground. They were bred to hunt vermin. The development of so many different types of terriers is a result of the geographical isolation of the areas in which they were bred. The Old English White Terrier, a breed that no longer exists, is thought to be the ancestor for most modern terriers. Many of the terriers and other essentially British dogs were later transported to Gaul and to the lands of the Mediterranean.

Breeds that can trace their ancestry back to this northern group include: Old English Sheepdog, Siberian Husky, Eskimo dog, Alaskan Malamute, Elkhound, Spitz, Welsh Corgi, Keeshond, Samoyed, and Chow Chow. The last two breeds were frequently used for food as well as for their hides. This can also be said of a number of the other large coated dogs.

THE MASTIFF GROUP

The *canis lupus chanco* or *laniger* describes the wolf group that served as the ancestors of the Mastiff group of dogs. These wolves lived in the mountain chain that links Europe and Asia. These mountains extend from China and Tibet in the East to Central Europe in the West, extending as far as the Pyrenees between France and Spain.

There undoubtedly were multiple ancestors for this group since the geographical area represented by this group was so vast. Because of this multiple parentage there is extreme variation as to size, shape, and color of individual specimens. The larger examples when first domesticated were used for herding and for hunting. Hunting in the early centuries of development would have been for such large game as the horse and the lion. Large dogs were also used as war animals. The largest Mastiff-like dogs were used by the hundreds along with the infantry in attacking enemy forces. They would be brought to the front of the line of march and then set free to attack the advancing enemy troops.

Descendants of these original Mastiff-type dogs are represented in at least six of the seven groups of modern dogs. In the Sporting Group they are represented by the Pointer, the Spaniel, the Setter, the Retriever, and the Weimaraner. In the Hound Group are included the Beagle, the Dachshund, the Fox Hound, the Harrier, and the Bloodhound.

The Working Group representatives are the Mastiff, the Bullmastiff,the Great Pyrenees, the Saint Bernard, the Newfoundland, the Komondorok, the Kuvaszok, and the Great Dane. The Terrier Group is represented by the Bull Terrier, which is a modern out-cross breed. In the Toy Group are the Pekingese, the Pug, the Japanese Chin, and the English Toy Spaniel. The Bulldog is the principal example found in the Non-Sporting Group. The Bulldog was a popular fighting dog in the Middle Ages and was used for baiting bulls and at times even lions. It was not until the eighteenth century that he became a popular house dog. The out-crosses of the Bulldog produced the Boxer, the French Bulldog, and the Bull Terrier. Also in the Non-Sporting Group is the Poodle.

THE GREYHOUND GROUP

The Greyhound group is a product of the *canis lupus pallipes* or the *canis lupus arabs*. These were, for the most part, coursing animals found in Africa and Arabia. Carvings have been found in Egypt that indicate that these types of dogs existed there for some five or six thousand years. These dogs were essentially sight hounds and were used for chasing down game in open country.

Modern breeds descending from these early dogs are the Greyhound, the Whippet, the Italian Greyhound, the Irish Wolfhound, the Scottish Deerhound, the Borzoi, the Afghan, and the Saluki. The Saluki is, perhaps, the oldest purebred dog in the world today. He was highly valued by the ancient Egyptians as a hunting dog. He was used to pursue gazelles, to catch them, and to hold them without killing them until the hunters arrived.

The Spotted Hyena, a native of central Africa.

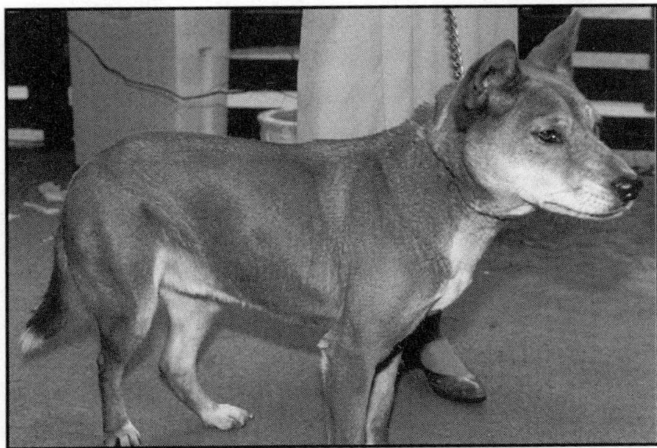

This Dingo is an atypical domesticated pet in Australia.

THE DINGO GROUP

The *canis lupus pallipes* also served as the common ancestor for the Dingo group of dogs. There was very little difference between this wolf and the pale-footed Asian wolf. These wolves ranged from the Middle East to the Far East, from Africa to Australia.

The present day Dingo carries certain physical characteristics of his wolf ancestor. These include the triangular-shaped head which facilitates his ability to see great distances. He has the flat brow, prick ears, and the low-carried tail. Like the wolf he carries his tail low covering his anus. This is thought to be a scent control for masking the odor from the anal glands. The Dingo like his early ancestor runs with his head erect as an aid to sighting game. The Dingo barks little as does the wolf.

The Dingo today is principally associated with Australia. There are at least two theories as to how the Dingo arrived in Australia. The first is that he was already there before Australia became separated from the Indian land mass. The other theory is that he was brought to the island-continent by early nomadic settlers when they arrived there in boats.

The Dingo is considered today the dog of the Australian aborigine. The Dingo was semi-domesticated by the aborigines from his feral state. The Dingo hunts in packs at night and has a dislike for man. This explains why there has been so little success in domesticating him. The Dingo existed in large numbers when the first European settlers discovered Australia in 1788.

The Dingo was the dog of the nomadic hunters. There is evidence that he existed in Australia more than fifteen centuries ago. During that time he has essentially reverted to his feral state. He is considered a pest by the modern inhabitants of Australia today because of his attacks on the sheep flocks. He is treated as a killer dog.

The other modern representatives of the Dingo Group are the Basenji and the Rhodesian Ridgeback, both native African dogs.

DOG AND MAN

Cave paintings found in Altamira, Spain, and in other caves in Spain and France indicate that a relationship existed between the dog and man for more than twelve thousand years. This mutual dependence came about as a result of the realization of a common need. Man needed the special herding and hunting talents of the dog, and the dog needed the protection and the food that man could provide. The dog served as a slave to the man-master and did what he was made to do. He worked for man and was fed by him.

Early dogs shared living quarters with man and lived in the same caves. They became allies as the dog helped man catch food. He later became the protector of the home and the flocks. As different types of flocks were cultivated, different types of dogs were needed. This led to the development of different breeds.

The scenting and herding abilities of the dog were important in driving wild animals into traps where they could be slaughtered by man. When the dog was not needed for hunting or herding he became the companion of man. In addition to being the guardian of the home and the flocks, the dog was also used as a draft animal.

Dogs used by desert tribes were the taller, long-legged varieties that could cope with the physical conditions found in a desert. Dogs used for hunting in jungles and forests were smaller so that they could move with less difficulty through the underbrush. When hunting became less of a need in the Middle Ages, the dog was used more for sport hunting by the rich.

EARLY DOGS

The earliest type of dog believed to have existed dates from some sixty million years ago. He was thought to have inhabited the lands between present-day Europe and Asia. The term Cynodictis is used to describe this specimen.

Fossil remains from forty million years ago indicate that the dog family existed at that time. The earliest specimen of a dog found in the Americas dates back some twenty-five million years. This dog's teeth were identical to those of the canis.

The Daphoenus was thought to be a link between the cat and the dog. He supposedly had the body of a cat and the head of a dog. He is said to have existed in North America some million years ago. The Mesocyn is claimed to be the link between the Daphoenus and the modern dog and also lived in North America.

Geographical isolation created the different groups of dog that exist today. Individual breeds were created by man to fulfill his own special needs. With little or no transportation and communication, little outside influence was exerted on these individual creations.

Dog breeding was already established in Neolithic times and the basic breeds of dogs were present then. Selective breeding was already understood at that time. The particular needs of a tribe or a clan dictated the type of dog that would be bred. Trade routes or migration routes eventually carried these individual breeds to new areas. Climate also dictated limits as to the type of dog that could survive in a particular area.

THE ANCIENT WORLD

As early as 3000 B.C. different types of dogs could be found in the burial tombs of the nobility. These types became more clear-cut during the next thousand years. Hunting dogs were used in the bas-relief carvings on tomb walls. Dogs were revered by the Egyptian nobility and were frequently put to death and embalmed along with their masters. Anubis is the dog- or jackal-headed God of Death in Ancient Egypt.

There were a number of different types of dogs in the ancient kingdom. These included the Maltese or small terrier-like dog, the hunting Pointer, the Basenji, the Mastiff, and the Greyhound. The Maltese dog was a member of the Spitz family and was much valued as a household pet in the region around the Mediterranean.

The peoples of the Eastern world captured the pariah dogs and then bred from them. Large, ferocious dogs were highly valued in India, China, and Tibet. These fierce hounds were descendants of the pale-footed Asian wolf. They were later crossed to the equally savage Indian Dholes. These large dogs were first used to guard the flocks and herds.

The smaller dogs were valued as household pets. Many of these dogs were developed in monasteries and were considered to be the protectors against evil spirits. These dogs included the Lhasa Apso, the Shih Tzu, and the Pekingese. These small dogs were only for the rich and as such were essentially city-type dogs.

Some thousand years ago the dog figured in mythology in Gaul and was used for sport hunting. The dog had become so popular by the Middle Ages in Europe that he was protected by law. He was a hunter of game and, therefore, an asset to his master. In Greece the Greyhound was used for sport hunting while toy dogs were considered to be ladies' dogs.

In prehistoric times a land bridge existed between Asia and North America. It is believed that the wolf traveled between the two continents over this land bridge and established himself in North America. Dogs played an important part in the religious ceremonies of the Aztecs in Mexico. In addition to their use by the church, dogs were also raised as an item of food and their hair and skin were of commercial value. These dogs were of a completely different type than those brought by the Spaniards in the sixteenth century. The Chihuahua is thought by some experts to be a native American dog. The other native American dog is the Bush Dog of Brazil. Effectively this dog is extinct today, but in the past he lived wild in the jungles of central South America.

In Ancient Rome the ownership of a dog was considered a privilege of the nobles. He was trained for whatever type of work that was needed. It was during this period that artificial qualities were first introduced into the dog.

The author Xenophon, who lived between 430 B.C. and 355 B.C., wrote a treatise with the title *Cynegetica* in which he discussed dogs. Aristotle, 384-322 B.C., discussed both wolves and dogs in his *Historia Animalium*. Varro, 82-27 B.C., described the dog as a protector of sheep and goats in his *De Rustica*. Pliny, 23-79 A.D., discussed the Mastiff-type war dogs that were used in fighting in his *History of the World*. Arrian, writing in the second century A.D., in his *Cynegeticus* described what must have been an early Irish Wolfhound as one of the Celtic dogs. Aelian, the second century Greek author, described the fierce dogs of India.

The Romans classified their dogs for either their physical qualities or for their working ability. These classifications included: the *Canes Villatici* which was the category for house dogs, the *Canes Pastorales Pecuarii* were the shepherd dogs, the *Canes Venatici* was for the sporting dogs, the *Canes Pugnaces* for the dogs used in war or for fighting in the arenas, the *Canes Nares* were the scent hounds, and the *Canes Pedibus Celeres* which were the sight hounds.

English writers began classifying dogs in the sixteenth century. This was mostly based on the function the dog served in society. These categories included hunting dogs, working dogs, and companion or non-sporting dogs. During the Renaissance, large dogs were used for hunting and small dogs were used as ratters or earth dogs which were used for burrowing. This latter category gave rise to the Terriers. Large dogs were also used as attack troops in battles. These dogs were starved prior to the battle to increase their motivation. In the arena, fighting dogs were also used to bait bulls, bears, and lions.

Man did not interfere with the breeding pattern of the wolf which explains why there are so few different types of wolves. Man did, on the other hand, interfere in the breeding of dogs, which has resulted in the large number of different breeds found throughout the world today.

In the nineteenth century new freedoms were granted to man in general and as a result hunting became a universal sport. This led to the breeding of special breeds with talents for a particular type of hunting. The controlled breeding programs along with the culling process led to the rapid development of many distinct and new breeds.

THE MODERN DOG

Religious cults have played an historical role in the development of certain modern breeds of dogs. The cult of the Lion was important in Buddhism in China, Tibet, Japan, and Korea. As the lion was the personification of Buddha, dogs that looked like a lion would also have religious importance. The Lion dogs, or Fo dogs, included the Lhasa Apso, the Pekingese, and the Shih Tzu. The golden color of the lion was extremely important. Carvings of the Fo dog are found throughout the Orient today. These dogs are always found in pairs. The male has one paw on a ball and the female is protecting a puppy. Ancestors of the Chow Chow as well as the Pekingese were present in China almost a thousand years ago. The excessively short nose of the Pekingese was much admired. This exaggerated nose was sometimes achieved by surgical means.

Moving westward from China, the Mastiff or Tibetan Mastiff was discovered. While these two modern breeds have a number of similarities they also have distinct differences. The Saluki was found farther to the West. He was a popular breed in Arabia and in Eastern Africa. Another African breed is the Basenji who was depicted in ancient Egyptian carvings. He is a descendant of the pale-footed Asian wolf.

The Spitz dog was found in the lands around the Mediterranean. One of the early examples of this breed is the Maltese that takes its name from the island of Malta. This dog was popular as a house pet in Egypt, Crete, Greece, and Rome. Early representations of this breed appear more Pomeranian in type. The Maltese was traded in Tibet under Buddhism and is believed to have played a role in the development of the Pekingese.

The Dalmatian was a dog of Mastiff origin and was brought by gypsies to eastern Europe. Herding and shepherd dogs were used in Hungary for these specific functions as well as guarding man and flock from wolves. These early dogs lead to the Komondorok, the Kuvaszok, and the Old English Sheepdog. Modern Terriers are for the most part the product of the British Isles. They are usually traced back to the Old English White Terrier which no longer exists.

There is a special category of dogs which is either endangered or already extinct. One of these dogs is the Peat Dog of central Europe. He lived some seven to eight thousand years ago and is thought to be the result of a cross between the jackal and the fox. The Dhole was the native dog of India. He was extremely ferocious and hunted in packs. The

Cape Dog from Southern Africa was also a breed that hunted in packs. He was large and had long legs. The Bush Dog of Brazil was a small, short-legged dog. Because of his isolation he appears little changed from earlier specimens.

With the establishment of the dog as an animal for sport, he also became a society-valued animal. The next logical step was for him to become a status symbol for man. When this happened it was only natural that man should give him qualities associated with man and with his society. This lead to the establishment of record keeping and informal competition. The next logical step from man's point of view was to establish more formal ways of recognition for man and his companion. This led directly to the formation of kennel clubs and dog show competition. The first established organization in this field was The Kennel Club of England, founded in 1859. This was followed by the Kennel Club of France in 1863 and the American Kennel Club in 1884.

Self-Test Questions

1. Which evolutionist writer did not believe the dog descended from the wolf?
2. Where did early paintings of the dog first appear?
3. What is the common Latin name for wolf?
4. Which strain of wolf produced the North American Eskimo dog?
5. Do both the dog and the wolf have strong territorial instincts?
6. What is scent marking?
7. What is the alpha dog?
8. Is there a difference in the gestation period for dogs and wolves?
9. Is the dentition of the dog and the wolf similar or different?
10. What is the scavenger dog?
11. What is a feral dog?
12. What is the pariah dog?
13. What are the four categories of the Northern Group?

Self-Test Questions

14. Which is the oldest breed of the Greyhound group?
15. Who domesticated the Dingo?
16. What are the two African representives of the Dingo group?
17. When did nobles start burying the dogs with their masters?
18. What breeds can trace their ancestry back to the northern group?
19. For how many years has there been a relationship between the dog and man?
20. What roles has the dog played in the life of man?
21. How many years ago did the earliest type of dog exist?
22. What was the Daphoenus?
23. What types of dogs were there in the ancient world?
24. What was the first kennel club to be founded, and when was it established?

Anatomy and Physiology of the Dog

Anyone seriously interested in the betterment of purebred dogs should be thoroughly familiar with all physical aspects of the dog. This is true whether the person is a breeder, a handler or a judge. These areas include the topology, the anatomy, and the physiology of the dog. Topology deals with the outside of the dog and is more commonly referred to as the points of the dog. These points are usually indicated by their common names and for the most part are familiar to all judges. The anatomy includes the study of both the skeletal system and the muscular system of the dog. Physiology is the study of the various parts of the dog and the relationship that exists between them and the functions that they perform.

POINTS OF THE DOG

Since the vocabulary for the points of the dog is a common one, it can readily be used in answering handlers' questions that refer to particular points of a dog. The following list includes those terms most commonly used in discussing and evaluating the dog.

Occiput — The occiput is the rearmost part of the skull. How prominent it is depends on the particular breed of dog. In some breeds it is quite easily seen while in other breeds it is felt rather than seen. The occiput helps in determining the shape of the head. It is the point of attachment for the brachiocephalicus muscle.

Ear — The placement of the ear on the side or on the top of the head helps in creating the expression of the dog

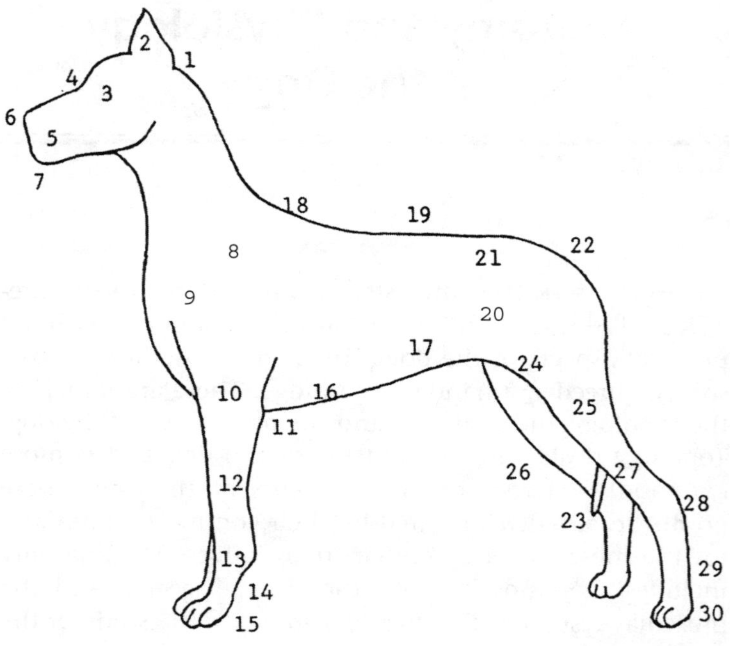

Points of the Dog

1. occiput	*16. brisket*
2. ear	*17. tuck-up*
3. eye	*18. withers*
4. stop	*19. back*
5. muzzle	*20. coupling*
6. nose	*21. loin*
7. mouth	*22. croup*
8. shoulder	*23. tail*
9. point of shoulder	*24. flank*
10. upper arm	*25. thigh*
11. elbow	*26. stifle*
12. forearm	*27. second thigh*
13. wrist	*28. hock*
14. pastern	*29. pastern*
15. paw	*30. paw*

by framing the face. High-set ears can give the impression that the head is deeper or longer than it really is while low-set ears can give the impression that the skull is wider than it actually is. The great flexibility of ear movement in some of the hound breeds adds to the alertness of their character. Incorrect ear placement is a fault in all breeds.

Eye — The eye is perhaps the single most important element in establishing the expression of a dog. Each breed has a correct or preferred eye shape, i.e. small, large, round, almond-shaped, triangular, etc. The wrong shape of the eye can give either too severe or too weak an expression. In addition there is the importance of the placement of the eye itself. Too close or too far apart, too low or too high in the skull and the expression is changed. Eye color is also an element of breed type.

Stop — The stop is the drop or break in the plane from the frontal bones of the skull to the nasal bones of the muzzle. The size or degree of the stop is an important element in analyzing the head shape. The stop is usually between the eyes and creates two separate planes of the head. The stop can be very great as is the case of the short-nosed breeds like the Shih Tzu and the Pekingese to virtually non-existent as is the case with the Borzoi and the Collie. The egg-shaped head of the Bull Terrier is still another example of one kind of stop.

Muzzle — The muzzle is that part of the head in front of the eyes. Its shape and length vary from breed to breed. The long, fine muzzle of the Saluki or the Afghan is in sharp contrast to the almost non-existent muzzle of the Pekingese, the Bulldog, or the Affenpinscher.

Nose — This refers to the external part of the nasal cavity. It includes the leather, the nostrils, and the septum. Sizes and shapes vary from breed to breed. The large nose of the Basset Hound contrasts with the small nose of the Brussels Griffon. The large open nostrils of the Bulldog are required because of the shortness of the nasal passage, while the long-muzzled dogs have proportionately smaller nostrils. Nose color is important as it serves as a point of disqualification in some breeds.

Mouth — The size and shape of the mouth is determined by the size and shape of the muzzle. The long mandible of the Borzoi allows space between the back teeth while the shortened muzzle of certain of the Toy breeds frequently causes jumbled teeth as there is not sufficient room for proper spacing. The length of the mandible also helps determine whether the breed will have a scissors bite, an even bite, or be undershot. Deviation from the standard serves as a frequent point of disqualification.

FOREQUARTERS

Shoulder — The shoulder of the dog consists of the scapula and the humerus and the common joint. The high point of the shoulder is the withers. The shoulder is of extreme importance in the movement of the dog as this construction is what determines the reach of the forward motion. The layback, or angle between the scapula and the humerus, facilitates or restricts the lift of the front leg. The layto, or the distance between the withers, determines the motion and flexion of the neck and head and can seriously affect the balance and the fluidity of the movement.

Point of Shoulders — The point of the shoulder is the shoulder joint itself. This is where the scapula and the humerus meet. This is the most forward point of the forequarters. It serves as a reference point in many breeds when making a comparison between height at the withers and length from point of shoulders to buttocks. The angle at the point of shoulder is a determiner in the movement of the dog.

Upper Arm — The upper arm is the part of the foreleg between the scapula and the radius or between the point of shoulder and the elbow. It is the humerus bone. The balance between the humerus and the scapula is one factor that determines the lift of the front legs. In the Miniature Pinscher the humerus often is shorter than the scapula which creates the hackney action of the breed. An imbalance between these two bones can cause faulty movement in any breed.

Elbow — The elbow is the joint between the humerus and the radius and ulna. Problems higher up in the shoulder are manifested in the placement of the elbow. A dog that is overloaded in shoulder will tend to be out at the elbows. A dog is said to be overloaded in shoulders when he has an excess buildup of muscles under the scapulae which forces them to spread apart at the tips. This creates a very loose movement and loss of efficiency. It can cause the dog to paddle or wing and depending on the construction of the rear can contribute to the crabbing motion of the dog.

Forearm — The forearm is that part of the foreleg between the elbow and the wrist. It consists of the radius and the ulna. The length of these bones varies with the breed as does their straightness or their curving. The forelegs of the Fox Terrier are very straight, while the forelegs of the Dachshund or the Basset Hound must curve to compensate for their shortness.

Wrist — The wrist is the collection of the carpal bones. It is these bones that give the flexibility to the pastern. Damage to this area is serious and affects the movement.

Pastern — The pastern is that section of the foreleg that contains the metacarpal bones. This is equivalent to the bones of the palm of a man's hand. The angle of the pastern helps to alleviate stress as the dog gallops. Coursing hounds have slightly sloping pasterns which help to diminish the stress as the foot strikes the ground at high speeds. The opposite of sloping pasterns is knuckling over and is a disqualification in the Basset Hound.

Paw — The paw contains the phalanges. These bones determine the shape of the foot, whether it is round and cat foot or long and hare foot. Since the phalanges of the dog are the fingers of man, the dog really stands on his fingers, so when it is stated that the dog is well up on toes, it means that he is really bearing his weight on his fingertips. The shape of the foot is determined by the moving function of the particular breed. A dog coursing in sand would need a longer foot for traction while a scent hound moving over rocks would need a smaller foot with thick pads that would aid with their gripping capabilities.

BODY

Brisket — The brisket is the lowest part of the chest cavity and corresponds to the area of the sternum. A dog that is described as having a deep brisket would be a coursing hound that would need a great deal of lung capacity for running. With the Dachshund the brisket must slope equally in both directions so that the dog can move easily in or back out of a tunnel without getting stuck.

Tuck-up — The tuck-up refers to the ascending line of the belly as it rises from the end of the rib cage to the hindquarters. This varies from breed to breed. There is very little tuck-up in the Golden Retriever but a great deal in the Whippet. A dog that moves at a sustained gallop will have more tuck-up than one that moves at a slower pace involving stops and starts and frequent turns.

Withers — The withers is that point on the topline of a dog where the neck and the back meet. It is where the scapulae and the first vertebrae of the thoracic spine meet. This point of anatomy is extremely important in movement so it is frequently referred to in standards. Some breeds call for little distance between the tips of the scapulae while others measure the distance in finger widths. The top of the withers is that point of a dog where height is determined.

Back — The back is that part of the topline of the dog that is limited to the thoracic vertebrae. It starts just behind the withers and continues to the loin of the dog. While the back is straight and level in most breeds there are some breeds that allow a sloping back. A back that is misshapen is listed among the faults in numerous breeds.

Coupling — The coupling refers to the area behind the end of the rib cage and the beginning of the hindquarters. The coupling determines the flexibility of the spinal movement. Some breeds are required to be short-coupled while others may be less so. This area is a factor in the freedom of movement.

Loins — The loins extend from the end of the rib cage to the beginning of the pelvis. It is the uppermost part of the area referred to as the coupling. Standards in numerous breeds call for some degree of rise over the loins. Other breeds require a straight line from behind the withers to the croup.

Tail — The tail is a continuation of the vertebral column and is made up of the coccygeal vertebrae. The tail contains from three to twenty-six bones. While some breeds have no tail, e.g. the Old English Sheepdog and the Pembroke Welsh Corgi, other breeds make use of their tails for balance while moving as is seen in the Belgians. The length, shape, and placement of the tail is one of the specifics in determining breed characteristics. Many breeds require the tail to reach the hock, while the Whippet's tail length is measured by drawing it between the legs and up the side of the dog to the iliac of the pelvis. The amount of feathering on the tail is important in the coated breeds, while the Labrador Retriever is required to have an otter-like tail.

Flank — The flank is the lowest area of the part referred to as the coupling. It is the fleshy underpart between the rib cage and the hindquarters. This is the area in which the tuck-up is seen.

HINDQUARTERS

Thigh — The thigh is that part of the hindquarters located between the hip joint and the knee joint. It includes the femur and the associated muscles. The angle between the femur and the pelvis, and the angle between the femur and the tibia and fibula is what determines the rear angulation of the dog. This in turn affects the rear action of the dog and establishes the movement. The bulk of musculature of the thigh is a characteristic of breed type.

Stifle — The stifle is the knee. It is that joint of the rear leg between the femur and the tibia and fibula. The angle at this joint helps to determine rear angulation. Many problems are associated with the stifle. Faults include being straight in stifle or having slipped stifles. Both of these problems have a serious effect on the rear action of the dog.

Second Thigh — The second thigh is also called the gaskin. In man it would be the lower leg. This is the area of the tibia and fibula and is located between the stifle and the hock. Some standards put particular emphasis on this part of the rear leg and the amount of muscle to be found there. The quality of the second thigh is reflected in the rear movement.

Hock — The hock is the joint of the rear leg located between the second thigh and the pastern. The bones of the hock are the tarsals. It would be equivalent to the ankle in man. The angle of the hock affects rear angulation and, therefore, the movement of the dog. Problems in the hock are common and are mentioned in many standards, e.g. cow hocks, sickle hocks, straight hocks, bow hocks. These all would cause general weakness in the rear and make the movement faulty.

Pastern — The rear pastern consists of the metatarsal bones and would be the equivalent of the foot of a man. It is normally at a ninety-degree angle to the ground in most breeds rather than being flat on the ground. Some standards call for this area to be well let down, which would mean that the pastern is to be short. Handlers frequently angle pasterns to lower the topline of the dog when it is high in rear because of poor angulation.

Paw — The paw contains the phalanges, bones which are the toes of the rear foot. The dog in most cases stands well up on toes if the dog has a cat-like foot. The dog with hare feet generally has a lower profile because of the angle of the second phalanges. In most breeds the shape and size of both the front and rear feet is the same, but there are some breeds in which the front and rear feet have a slightly different shape and are even of a different size.

SKELETAL SYSTEM

The skeleton of the dog gives him his overall size and shape and in addition gives protection to the internal organs. All dogs have the same number of bones in their bodies excepting the tail which varies in length depending on the docking. Since the tail may have as few as three bones and as many as twenty-six, the total number of bones in the body will reflect this difference.

There are basically two parts to the skeletal system. The first is the axial skeleton which contains the bones of the skull, the spine including the tail, the rib cage, and the pelvis. These bones are irregular in shape such as the bones of the skull and the vertebrae, or are flat as are the ribs and the sternum. The appendicular skeleton includes the bones of the fore and hind legs. These bones are cylindrical in shape and are classified as long or short.

Skull

The skull not only refers to the part of the head behind the eyes but includes all the bones that make up the head. This includes not only the fourteen fused bones which make up the cranium that protects the brain, but also the thirty-six fused bones that form the muzzle.

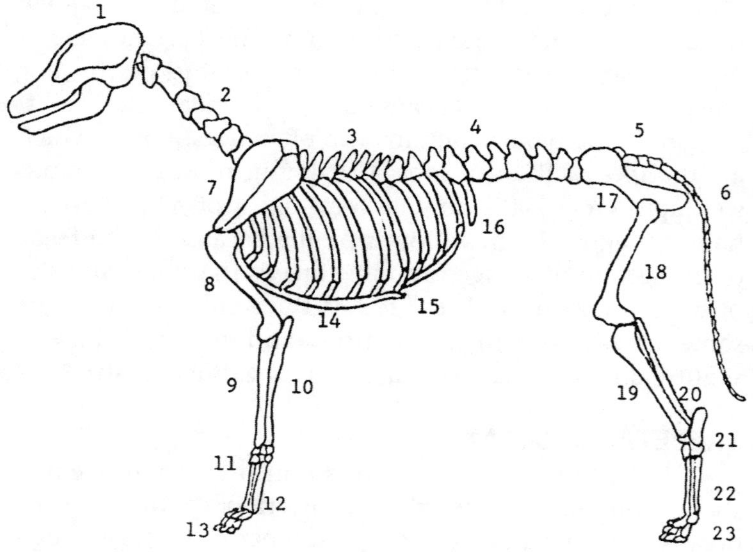

Skeleton of the Dog

1. *skull*
2. *cervical spine*
3. *thoracic spine*
4. *lumbar spine*
5. *sacral spine*
6. *coccygeal spine*
7. *scapula*
8. *humerus*
9. *radius*
10. *ulna*
11. *carpus*
12. *metacarpus*
13. *phalanges*
14. *sternum*
15. *xiphoid*
16. *ribs*
17. *pelvis*
18. *femur*
19. *tibia*
20. *fibula*
21. *tarsus*
22. *metatarsus*
23. *phalanges*

Thirty-four of these thirty-six bones are paired with one on each side of the muzzle. The remaining two bones are unpaired. These two bones are very different in size and shape from all the other bones of the skull.

Since the bones of the skull are fused, they are individually indistinguishable in a hands-on examination of the head. Some others, however, are important in evaluating the length and width of the head and in determining the correct shape and proportions. The occiput is the rearmost point of the skull and is the end of the occipital crest which is formed by the joining of the parietal bones of the sides of the head. In some breeds this point is mentioned in the standard and is easily seen. In other breeds this point is not mentioned. The occiput must be checked with the hands.

The zygomatic arch forms the cheek bone of the dog. It rises at approximately the level of the opening of the ear and is fused to the maxilla bone below the eye. This bone forms the bony orbit at the underside of the eye. It also serves as the anchor and hinge for the mandible. The zygomatic arch can be thick and full as is the case in the Bulldog, giving roundness to the cheeks, or it can be flat and more streamlined as is the case in the Borzoi.

The mandible is the lower jaw. Its length and width is determined by the type of skull. It is the mandible that determines whether or not a dog will have a scissors bite, an even bite, or be undershot. The width of the jaw will influence the alignment of the teeth. If the mandible is narrow there may not be enough room for the six incisors and therefore the the teeth may not be in a perfect row, but rather be jumbled or out of line. In some cases when the jaw is narrow there may be fewer than six incisors. The mandible works on a hinge joint and moves when the dog is chewing.

The maxilla is the upper jaw and is the fixed and fused bone of the muzzle. It does not move at all and chewing is

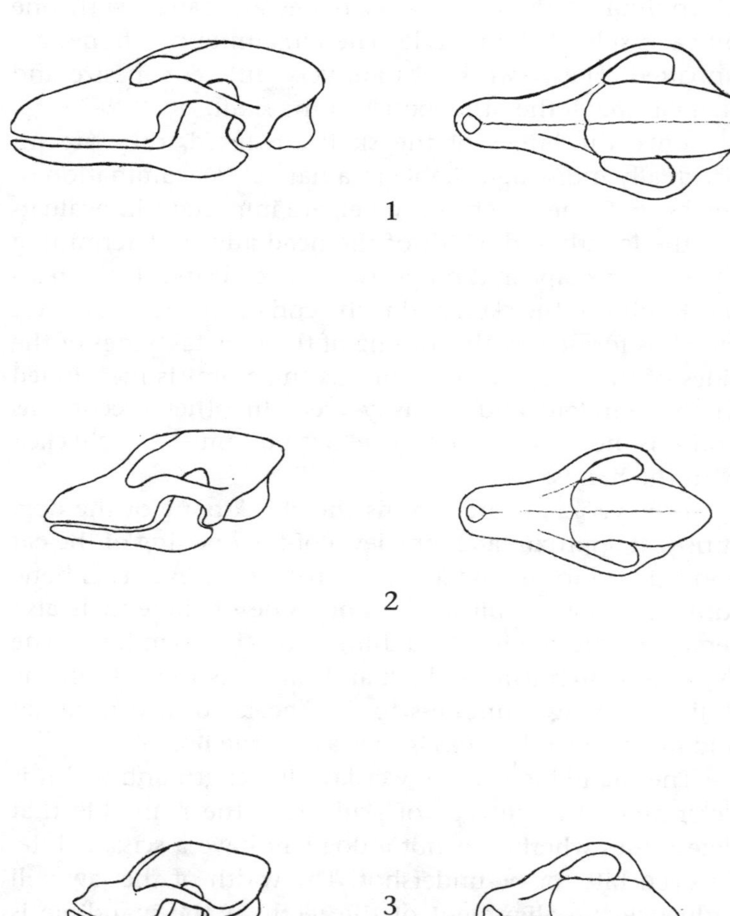

Skull Shapes: 1. dolichocephalic 2. mesoticephalic 3. brachycephalic

carried out solely by the action of the mandible. The maxilla is fused to the zygomatic arch and forms part of the orbit for the eye. The length and width of the maxilla determines the skull type.

There are three types of skull. They are classified by their length and width. The long, narrow skull is the dolichocephalic. The very short, wide skull is the brachycephalic and the mesoticephalic skull is medium in both length and width. The Borzoi and the Saluki would be examples of the dolichocephalic type. The Bulldog and the Pekingese would be examples of the brachycephalic skull while the Siberian Husky and the Tibetan Terrier would be examples of the mesoticephalic skull.

Dentition

Dentition is the term used to describe the bite of the dog together with the individual teeth, their size and their shape, and the placement of the teeth in the jaws. Dentition comes from the Latin word *dens* for tooth.

The puppy is born without teeth but the teeth begin to appear at about three to four weeks of age. The first teeth to erupt are the canines. These are the holding teeth and there are four of them. There are six incisors in both the lower and upper jaw and they are located between the canines. Behind the canines are the premolars, three on each side both upper and lower, for a total of twelve. The total complement of puppy teeth is twenty-eight.

The adult teeth begin to replace the puppy teeth when the dog is about four or five months old. All the puppy teeth will be replaced but there will also be some additional teeth in the adult dog. This will include an additional premolar on each side of both jaws. In addition there will be two molars on each side of the upper jaw and three on each side of the lower jaw. This gives a total of forty-two teeth in the adult dog.

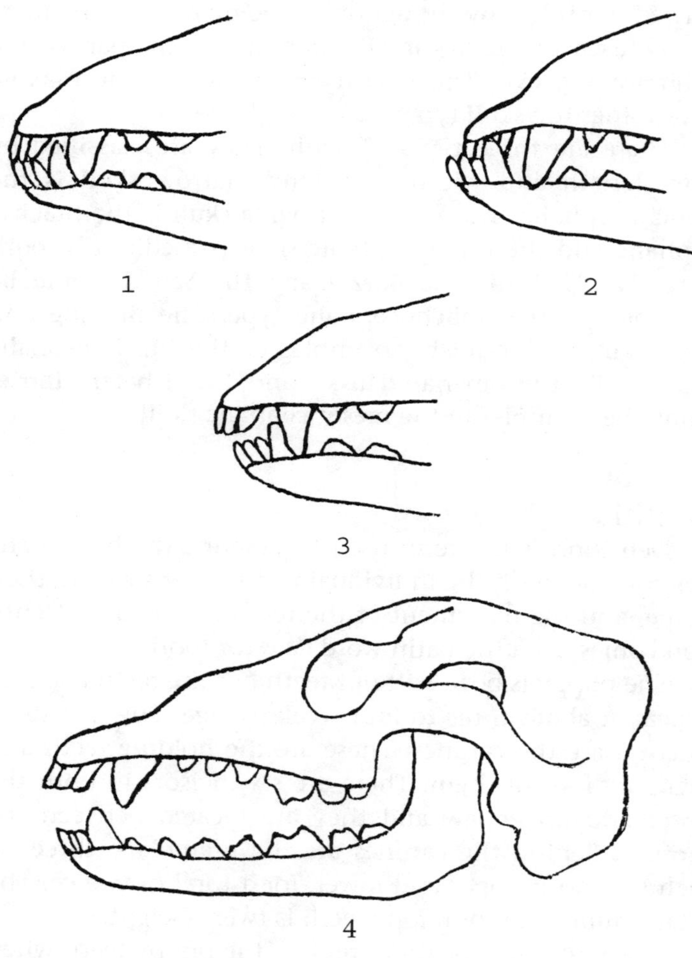

Dentition

1. *scissors bite*
2. *undershot bite*
3. *overshot bite*
4. *complete dentition—upper: 6 incisors, 2 canines, 8 premolars, 4 molars; lower: 6 incisors, 2 canines, 8 premolars, 6 molars.*

A total of 42 teeth.

A number of breed standards do not mention teeth at all either as to number or placement. There are a few standards which do not even mention if the bite is to be scissors, even, or undershot. It is assumed that the judge has sufficient knowledge to be able to supplement the standard.

Dentition is a problem in a number of breeds and the lack of the correct number of teeth is mentioned as a disqualification in several breeds. Some of the working breeds indicate that there has perhaps been an historical problem with dentition since a penalty of disqualification has been established for such breeds as the Doberman Pinscher and the Rottweiler. The Doberman standard calls for disqualification if there are four or more missing teeth, and the Rottweiler if there are two or more missing teeth.

Standards use three terms to describe acceptable bites. They are the scissors bite in which the inner edge of the upper incisors is just in front of and touching the outer edge of the lower incisors. The even bite describes a mouth in which the bottom edge of the upper incisors rests directly on top of the top edge of the lower incisors. The undershot bite is one in which the inner edge of the lower incisors is just beyond the outer edge of the upper incisors. If this is a very tight or close bite, it is sometimes described as a reverse scissors bite.

While the undershot bite is called for in some standards such as the Bulldog and the Lhasa Apso, it is considered a fault in other breeds. There are degrees of being undershot and there are degrees of being overshot so careful consideration must be given to this problem. Some standards list an exact measurement for being overshot. The Whippet standard, for example, lists as a disqualification a bite that is more than one-quarter of an inch overshot.

Many of the standards for breeds in the United States were taken directly from the standards used by the Kennel Club in England. In the English standards the word *level* was frequently used in describing the mouth. In these standards the term *level* was used to describe the evenness of the height of the teeth and the similar length of the jaws. It did not refer to the bite of the dog. Therefore a level bite was not synonymous with an even bite. This was misunderstood by the writers of a number of the standards in the United States and it is now accepted by many breeders and judges that *level* means *even*. Another term used to describe the even bite is the Pincer bite.

While it is not mentioned in standards, the wry mouth is unacceptable. A wry mouth is caused by out-of-line teeth which prevent the jaw from closing in the normal manner, or it is the result of a congenital deformity in the jaw itself. In either case it is unacceptable. A dog with a wry mouth in the natural state would not survive for long as he would be unable to provide sufficient food for himself. The constant use of crooked teeth would cause them to break and he would, therefore, not be able to hunt.

Spine

The spinal or vertebral column consists of thirty vertebrae not counting the coccyx or the coccygeal vertebrae since the number of bones here can vary from breed to breed because of docking. No two bones are alike and none is paired with any other. The vertebrae are separated from each other by the intervetebral discs which are cartilaginous. These discs allow limited movement of the vertebrae and also act as shock absorbers. Damage to these discs can have serious consequences in the movement of the dog.

The cervical spine consists of seven vertebrae and begins at the base of the skull. The first two of these bones are different in function and general shape from the rest. The first vertebra is called the atlas and is somewhat doughnut shaped. The second vertebra is called the axis and has a bony spur or column that projects up through the hole in the atlas. This serves as a pivot point and allows the dog complete freedom to move his head from side to side and allows more restricted motion in moving head up and down. Starting with the fourth vertebrae there arises a small bony projection called the spinous process which increases slightly in length with each succeeding vertebra.

The thoracic spine consists of thirteen vertebrae. There is a great increase in the length of the spinous process starting with the first thoracic vertebra. The first four are the longest and point almost straight up. This is the area of top attachment for the scapula and forms the withers of the dog. The spinous process of next five vertebrae decrease successively in size and begin to slant toward the rear. This is what causes the slight dip in the topline behind the withers. The spinous process on the remaining four vertebrae is shorter and thicker. On the lower side of each thoracic vertebrae is attached one of the pairs of the ribs. The back of the dog begins at about the fifth vertebra and runs to the lumbar spine.

The lumbar spine consists of seven vertebrae. The spinous process on each of these vertebrae is shorter and thicker and gradually points towards the head of the dog in the rear portion of the lumbar spine. This area corresponds to the loin of the dog.

The sacral spine or the sacrum of the dog consists of three fused vertebrae. Since these bones are fused there is not even limited movement. The sacrum forms part of the croup and serves as the point of attachment for the pelvis. Since the pelvis is fused to the sacrum it is considered part of the axial spine. It is also part of the croup.

The coccygeal spine is the tail of the dog. The number of bones varies in this part of the spine. There are at least three deep vertebrae even in the tailless breeds and there may be as many as twenty-six bones in tails as long as the tail of the Scottish Deerhound. A number of standards call special attention to the function of the tail when the dog

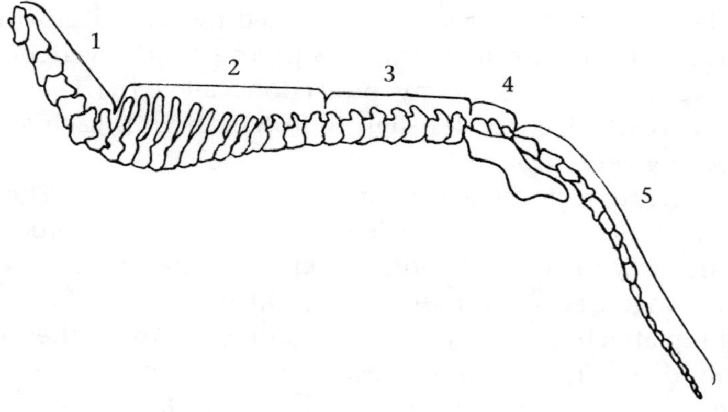

Spine of the Dog

1. *cervical vertebrae*
2. *thoracic vertebrae*
3. *lumbar vertebrae*
4. *sacral vertebrae*
5. *coccygeal vertebrae*

is moving. The tail is of special importance in the short-coupled herding breeds as it aids the dog in balance when he is making short turns at high speed.

Rib Cage

The rib cage gives shape to the chest and protection to the vital organs contained therein. There are thirteen pairs of ribs each joined to one of the thirteen thoracic vertebrae. The thoracic spine is on the top, the ribs are on the side, and the sternum joins the ribs at the bottom and determines the size and shape of the rib cage. The sternum is a long, flat bone and is vital in the production of red blood cells. The first nine pairs of ribs are joined directly to the sternum. The next three pairs are each joined at the tip to the preceding rib which in turn is joined to the ninth pair of ribs. The thirteenth pair of ribs is joined only to the spinal vertebra and these ribs are not joined at the bottom. They are sometimes called floating ribs for this reason.

The sternum is sometimes referred to as the breastbone or the brisket. It is also referred to as the keel, being the lowest part of the chest. The sternum is a series of fused bones and is basically divided into three sections. The foremost part is called the prosternum or the manubrium. This part of the sternum projects beyond the attachment of the first rib and is easily seen in those breeds which have a prominent forechest. In those breeds which do not have such a forechest, it can easily be felt. It is located at about the height of the point of shoulders. The point of shoulders is where the scapula and the humerus meet. The middle part of this bone is simply called the sternum and the rearmost part is called the xiphoid process. This is a cartilaginous projection and can be felt just behind the point where the ninth ribs join the sternum.

Forequarters

The forequarters and the hindquarters are collectively described as the running gear of the dog. The forequarters consist of the scapula, the humerus, the radius, the ulna, the carpus, the metacarpus, and the phalanges.

The scapula in man is called the shoulder blade. It is attached to the thoracic spine by muscles. The point where the scapula joins the spine is called the withers and is the highest point of the topline. It is at this point that the dog is measured to determine his height. In most breeds the ideal layback of the shoulder or scapula is said to be forty-five degrees from the horizontal. The angle at which the scapulae meet the spine at the withers is described as the layto. Some standards are precise in establishing the distance between the tips of the scapulae, some calling for little space and others specifying the distance between these two bones by the width of a certain number of fingers.

The humerus is also called the upper arm. The foremost part of the forequarters is called the point of shoulders which is the point where the scapula and the humerus meet in a hinge joint. The point of shoulders is one of the landmarks used in determining the balance between the height of the dog and his length. In the ideal dog the angle where the humerus meets the scapula is ninety degrees. Many dogs do not meet this ideal standard. At the lower end, the humerus is joined to the forearm with a hinge joint.

The forearm consists of the radius and ulna. The radius is the shorter and heavier of the two bones. It is the more forward of the two. The ulna is the rear bone and the longer one. The topmost part of the ulna is called the olecranon. It extends past the top of the radius and serves as the point of attachment for some muscles of the shoulder. The shape of these bones determines the shape of the forelegs as to whether they are round, oval or flat. While these bones are normally straight, certain standards allow for foreshortening of these bones and for curvature so that they may wrap around the rib cage in a breed like the Dachshund. The joint between the humerus and the forearm is the elbow and the joint between the forearm and the pastern is the carpus or the wrist.

The carpus consists of the seven carpal bones assembled more or less in a two-tiered arrangement. These bones of the wrist give great flexibility of motion, allowing the dog to move the pastern through a wide range of field.

The pastern or metacarpus consists of the five metacarpal bones. Four are of equal length and the fifth one, which is equivalent to the thumb in man, forms the dewclaw. The angle at which the pastern meets the horizontal plane varies with the breed. In some breeds they are more or less upright, as in the Harrier, and in other breeds they have considerable slope, as is seen in the case of the German Shepherd.

The phalanges are the bones of the foot. These bones are the same ones that are the fingers in man. The four toes of the dog each have three phalanges while only two are attached to the fifth metacarpal or the dewclaw. The phalanges that are attached to the metacarpals are the longest of the three sets and should be parallel to the ground. The second phalanges slope down toward the ground at about a forty-five-degree angle in the cat foot, and in the hare foot these bones meet the horizontal plane at about a thirty-degree angle. The short phalanges in front that actually touch the ground are the true toes and contain the toenail.

Hindquarters

The hindquarters are the rear running gear of the dog. This consists of the femur, the tibia, the fibula, the tarsus, the metatarsus, and the phalanges.

The femur is the thigh bone and forms the hip joint where it meets the pelvis. This is a ball-and-socket joint and has greater freedom of movement than does the hinge joint. At the lower end it forms the stifle or knee joint where it meets the tibia and fibula. The femur is a very strong, thick bone as it is a major weight-carrying bone. The angle that the femur makes where it meets the pelvis should match the angle of the shoulder if the dog is to be balanced and move correctly. When one of these angles is greater than the other, the dog will have faulty movement. When a dog is diagnosed as being dysplastic, it is the hip joint that is affected.

The stifle is the knee joint and is of the hinge type. The stifle joint consists of ligaments and includes the patella or knee cap. A slipped stifle, which is also called patellar subluxation, describes the condition in which the knee cap is not maintained in its proper location and moves around, causing the dog to skip a step when he is gaiting. Another condition that causes faulty movement is when the dog is said to be too straight in stifle. This means that the angle is too great and the dog will have weak rear drive and take shorter steps than he should. Many standards call for the stifle to be well bent while other standards say the dog has a good turn of stifle.

The tibia and fibula form the second thigh, which is also called the gaskin in some breeds. The second thigh is equivalent to the lower leg in man. Both of these bones are of the same length, but the tibia is a thick, strong bone while the fibula has a very small diameter. The angle of the stifle and the length of the tibia and fibula decide whether or not the dog will have good or correct angulation or be over-angulated.

The hock is the ankle joint and is formed where the tibia and fibula meet the tarsus. This angle along with the angle at the stifle determines whether or not the dog will have the correct angulation. Many standards call for the hock to be well let down which means that the pasterns should be short.

The tarsus is a collection of bones that form the ankle. There are seven of these bones and they have a similar arrangement to the carpus in that they are in two rows. Injury to either the carpus or tarsus could cause the dog to become crippled. There must be good flexibility in this joint if the dog is to have rear drive.

The metatarsals are the bones of the rear pastern. There are five of these bones, but the one that forms the dewclaw is very short and has no significance except in a breed like the Briard which calls for the dog to be disqualified if this appendage is absent. When the standard calls for short hocks it really means that the metatarsals are to be short. When these bones are long, they result in weak rear drive since the flexing of longer bones is less efficient when the dog moves at even a moderate speed.

The phalanges are the bones of the rear foot and have a description that is essentially the same as that of the foot of the front leg. They form the paw and determine whether the foot will be cat-shaped or hare-shaped or something in between.

MUSCLE SYSTEM

The skeletal system gives the dog his shape and form and protects the internal organs. The muscle system allows the dog to move the bones and thus provides his capability of movement. The study of the muscle system is called myology. To understand how the muscle system works, one must understand what a muscle is and what causes it to contract and relax, for this is the action that moves the bones when a dog is gaiting.

There are three types of muscles: smooth muscle, cardiac muscle, and skeletal muscle. Smooth muscles are found in the walls of the hollow organs and in blood vessels. Smooth muscles are distinguished from the other two types in that they are smooth and not striated as are the cardiac and skeletal muscles. (Striated muscles are threadlike muscles as seen under a microscope.) These are involuntary muscles and are part of the autonomic nervous system and thus beyond the voluntary control of the dog. These muscles are also under hormonal influence. Cardiac muscles form the bulk of the heart itself. These muscles are striated and are under the control of the autonomic nervous system, which categorizes them as involuntary.

The fibers of the skeletal muscles are long, cylindrical cells. They are very long in comparison to the smooth muscles which run from 15 to 500 microns. (One micron is one thousandth part of one millimeter and there are one thousand millimeters in one meter which is 39.37 inches long.) Skeletal muscles can be as long as four centimeters which would be 40,000,000 microns long. The smooth muscle fibers are about 6 microns in diameter while striated muscles can be between 10 and 100 microns in diameter. These muscles are striated and not smooth.

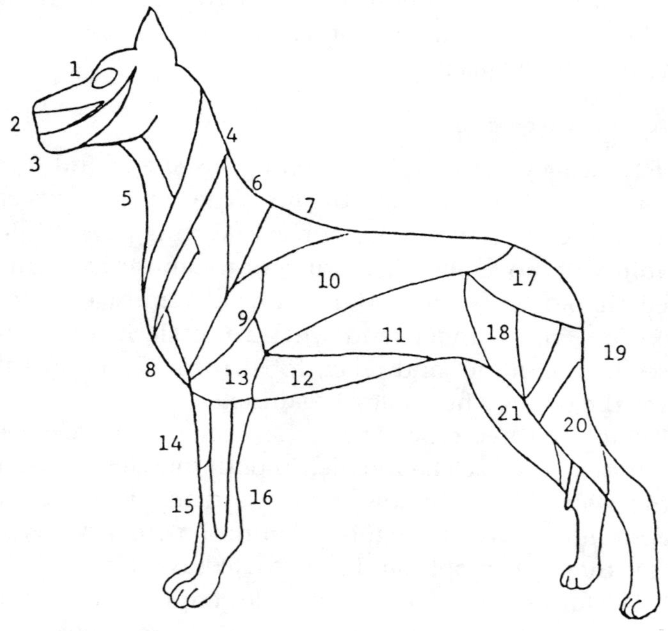

Muscle System

1. *orbicular oculi*
2. *levator nasolabialis*
3. *zygomaticus*
4. *brachiocephalicus*
5. *sterno-hyoideus*
6. *trapezius*
7. *trapezius*
8. *brachiocephalicus*
9. *deltoid*
10. *latissimus dorsi*
11. *obliquus abdominis externus*
12. *posterior deep pectoral*
13. *triceps*
14. *extensor carpi radialis*
15. *extensor carpi obliquus*
16. *flexor carpi ulnaris*
17. *gluteus medius*
18. *tensor fasciae latae*
19. *gluteus superficialis*
20. *biceps femoris*
21. *sartorius*

They are voluntary muscles and are under the control of the dog.

The muscle is made up of muscle fibers. The smallest segment of a muscle fiber is the sarcomere. As seen in the illustration, the sarcomere is made up of two types of mylofilaments: actin, which is the thin filament, and myosin, which is the thick filament. While neither of these two filaments is capable of contracting, their arrangement does allow the actin to slide past the myosin and shorten the total length of the sarcomere by about a third of its original length. When all the sarcomeres in line do the same thing, the muscle itself contracts and in so doing causes the bone to be pulled in the direction of the contracting muscle. The compensatory or paired muscle relaxes at the same time, thus releasing tension on the bone and allowing for the smooth, coordinated movement of the bone. These muscles must work in unison or there can be no movement.

Sarcomere
In a relaxed state.
1. H zone. 2. I band. 3. A band 4. Thin myofilament
5. Thick myofilament

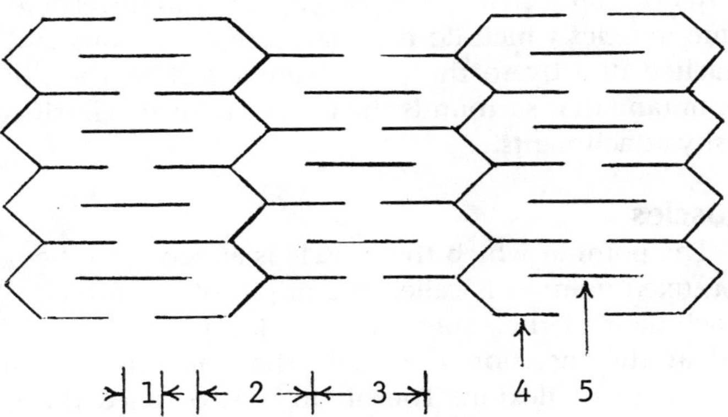

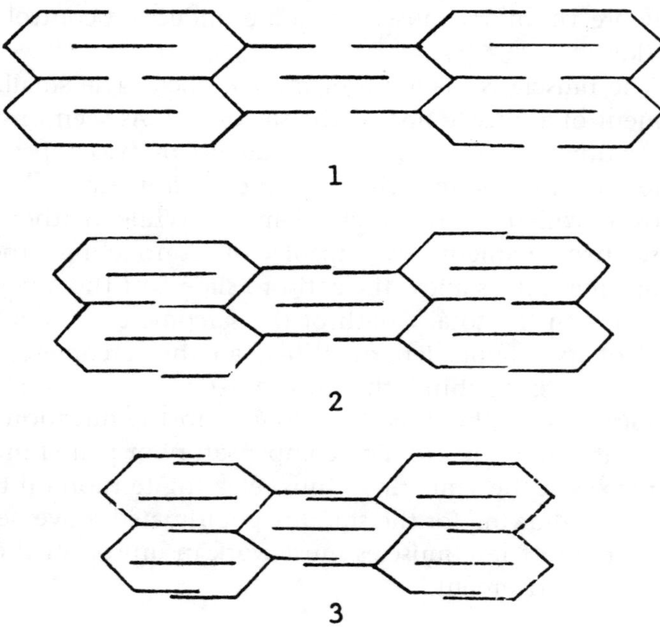

Sarcomere
1. Muscle cell relaxed. 2. Muscle cell partially contracted.
3. Muscle cell contracted (shortened).

The skeletal muscles are attached to the bones by segments of connective tissue called the tendons. There are some muscles which do not make use of tendons and are attached directly to the periosteum which is the fibrous membrane that surrounds the bone. These are classified as fleshy attachments.

Muscles

The point at which the muscle is attached to the bone in a fixed manner is called the origin of the muscle. The attachment of the other end is called the insertion. The end at the insertion is usually the one that has more movement or flexion. The origin is also called the head and is normally the more proximal of the two points of attachment. (Proximal means near the center of the body and distal means away from the center of the body.) The fleshy part of the muscle itself is the segment which contracts and relaxes and is called the belly which is well supplied with blood. This contracting and relaxing is what changes the total length of the muscle. When the muscle becomes shorter the bone is pulled toward its origin, and when it relaxes the bone is no longer held under tension and is allowed to move away from its origin and toward its insertion. Fan-like muscles that are broad may have more than one origin and more than one insertion.

The muscles contract and relax when a nerve impulse travels through the neurofibrils, which is the nerve network of the body, and arrives at the neuromuscular spindles, which are the receptors for such impulses in the skeletal muscles. This nerve impulse programs the muscle to react in an appropriate manner.

While it would be ideal for a judge to have a complete command of the muscle system of the dog so that he might fully understand the entire structure and function of the dog, it would require years of concerted study in a school of veterinary medicine or under special study with a veterinarian. While this would be ideal, it is just not possible for most individuals. What a judge must have at his command is a thorough working knowledge of the superficial muscle system, for these are the muscles that he can feel on the physical examination of the dog. These terms are useful to the judge when he is called upon to analyze physical problems of a specific dog. Most exhibitors may not be familiar with the correct terminology. This lack of knowledge on the part of the exhibitor affords the judge an opportunity to provide continuing education. By using common, specific, and correct terminology a detailed and scientific analysis can be made of an individual physical problem.

Muscles of the Head

Muscles give both form and substance to the head and provide the ability to move the jaw. The sheet of muscles that covers the top half of the muzzle is called the levator nasolabialis muscle. The muscles that form a semicircle around the upper and lower lips are the orbicularis oris. Perhaps the most important muscle of the head is the zygomaticus, which is attached to the skull just in front of the opening of the ear canal and runs down the cheek and the length of the lower jaw. This muscle gives motion to the lower jaw for both holding and chewing. The muscles of the forehead are the scutuloauricularis superficialis, which are an extension of the frontalis. The muscles that form the orbit for the eye are the orbicularis oculi. The last major superficial muscle of the head, the platysma, extends from the rear of the upper and lower jaw and sweeps broadly up to the cervical spine.

Muscles of the Head

1. Levator nasolabialis 2. Orbicularis oculi 3. Frontalis 4. Zygomaticus 5. Zygomaticoauricularis 6. Orbicularis oris 7. Platysma

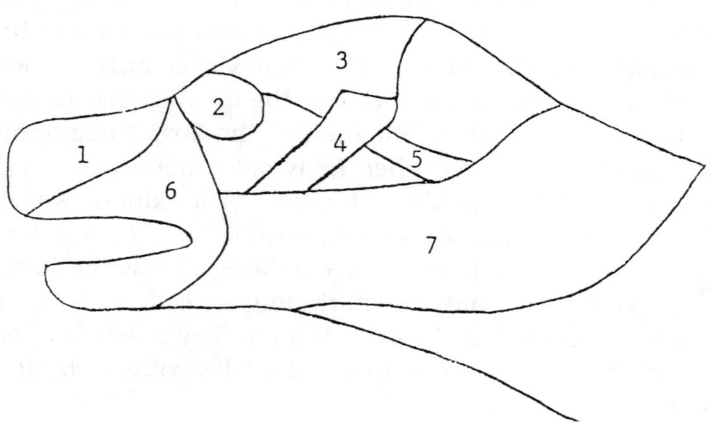

Muscles of the Neck and Forequarters

The brachiocephalicus is a broad muscle that starts just behind the occiput. It extends down the first part of the cervical spine and then swings down in a narrowing triangle band and is attached to the forearm. The two muscles on the underside of the neck which extend from the base of the skull to the sternum are the sternothyroideus on the top and the sternohyoideus on the bottom.

Starting up on the cervical spine where the brachiocephalicus muscle ends and moving down to the point of withers is the trapezius muscle. It descends down the spine of the scapula and then back up to the crest of the cervical spine and thus takes on a broad, fan-like shape. The trapezius is a paired muscle. The second half is attached to the rear side of the spine of the scapula and extends in triangular shape up to the thoracic spine. When one side of the trapezius contracts, the other half relaxes to work in perfect harmony, allowing back-and-forth motion.

The deltoideus joins the bottom half of the scapula to the top half of the humerus. Immediately behind this muscle is the triceps which joins the lower half of the scapula to the bottom half of the humerus and the top part of the ulna. The biceps joins the top half of the humerus to the top half of the radius. These muscles that connect bones on either side of a joint give the opening and closing capability to that joint. The external carpi radialis runs from the lower end of the humerus to the bottom of the radius. The ulnaris lateralis joins the lower end of the humerus to the lower part of the ulna. The topmost part of the ulna is called the olecranon. The muscles joining it to the humerus above is the anconeus and to the radius below is the flexor carpi ulnaris.

Muscles of the Back

There is a broad triangular sheet of muscles extending the length of the thoracic and lumbar spines that is

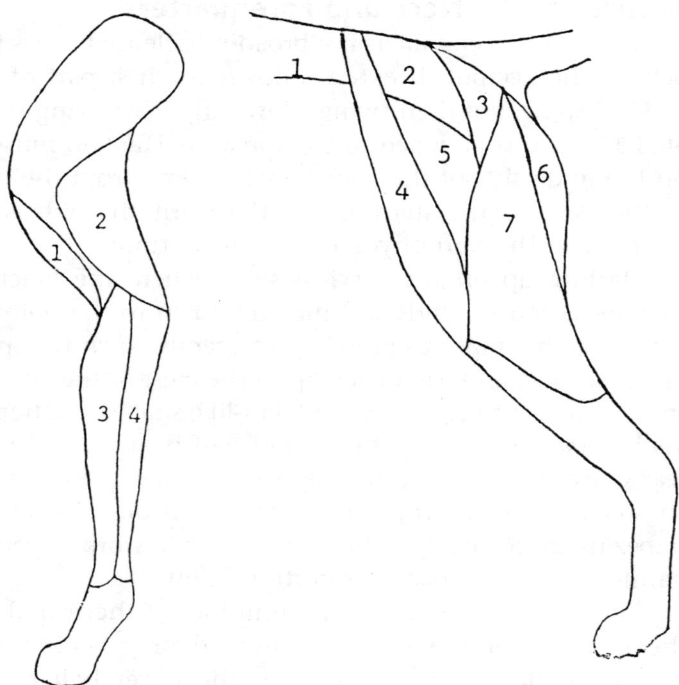

Muscles of the Forequarters

1. *biceps*
2. *triceps*
3. *extensor carpi radialis*
4. *extensor carpi ulnaris*

Muscles of the Hindquarters

1. *longissimus dorsi*
2. *gluteus medius*
3. *gluteus superficialis*
4. *cranial sartorius*
5. *fascia lata*
6. *semitendinosus*
7. *biceps femoris*

attached to the forequarters in front. This is the latissimus dorsi. Another fan-like muscle connecting the lower edges of the ribs to the hindquarters is the obliquus abdominis externus. The posterior deep pectoral muscles follow along the keel and underbelly between the forequarters and the hindquarters. The superficial pectoral muscles link the humerus and the sternum. The longissimus dorsi runs the length of the thoracic and lumbar spinal column and gives form and strength to the entire vertebral column.

Muscles of the Hindquarters

The middle gluteal muscles join the lumbar spine to the pelvis while the superficial gluteal muscles join the pelvis to the femur. The semitendinosus muscles join the rear of the pelvis to the tibia and their bulk forms the buttocks. The tensor fascia lata connects the lumbar spine to the femur. The cranial sartorius joins the front of the pelvis to the lower end of the femur and the upper end of the tibia. The biceps femoris is attached to the rear of the pelvis and extends down in triangular shape to the tibia. This muscle forms the bulk of the upper thigh.

The top extension of the hock or ankle joint is the os calcis. This bone is connected up to the biceps and the femur by the tendon of gastrocnemius. This is popularly called the Achilles tendon and injury to this tendon can have a crippling effect on the dog.

There are many other muscles that play important roles in the movement of the dog. These are the extensor and flexor muscles that work in harmony with each other and that allow the dog to move a specific part of a limb. These muscles for the most part are deeper muscles and only a few can be easily palpated, so for this reason they have not been included in this analysis. There are many reference books available for those interested in pursuing this phase of the muscle system in greater depth.

Self-Test Questions

1. What is topology?
2. What is anatomy?
3. What is kinesiology?
4. What are the two most important elements in expression?
5. Where is the stop located?
6. Where is the point of shoulders located?
7. What is the name of the bone that is commonly called the shoulder blade?
8. What is the name of the bone that comprises the upper arm?
9. What are the two bones of the forearm?
10. What are the bones of the wrist?
11. What are the bones of the front pastern?
12. What are the bones of the paw?
13. Where is the height of a dog measured?
14. What bones make up the hock joint?

Self-Test Questions

15. What bones make up the rear pastern?
16. What are the two divisions of the skeleton?
17. What is the rearmost part of the skull called?
18. What are the three head shapes?
19. What are the five divisions of the spine?
20. What is the upper thigh bone called?
21. What are the two bones of the lower thigh?
22. What is the study of the muscle system called?
23. What does the tuck-up refer to?
24. What is the shape of the foot determined by?
25. What does the coupling determine on a dog?
26. What purpose does the zygomatic arch serve in a dog?
27. How many teeth does the adult dog have?
28. What three terms are used in standards to describe acceptable bites?

Movement

The judge must evaluate the dog when it is standing still and when it is moving. When the dog is standing in a comfortable pose he will not have to adjust his feet or move. When the dog is in this position he is said to have static balance. This means that his legs act as columns of support for his body weight. His legs will be four-square and give a base that is in correct balance for his length, width, and height.

STATIC BALANCE

The center of static balance of the forequarters is located at a midpoint on the scapula, about halfway down the center spine. A line dropped from this point down to form a perpendicular angle with the ground could be called the line of static balance for the forequarters. Viewed from the front in the majority of dogs that do not have an overly developed chest, this line would pass down the inside of the humerus and the radius and ulna bones and just on the inside of the paw. In a very narrow-chested dog this line might even pass through these bones and through the middle of the paw. This would not be as strong a front as it would cause the base of the dog to be too narrow. By coming just to the inside of the front legs the base is wider and the pectoral muscles will supply the tension to strengthen the columns of support for the dog.

If the dog is extremely wide-chested or bull-chested, the static line of balance will be greatly removed toward

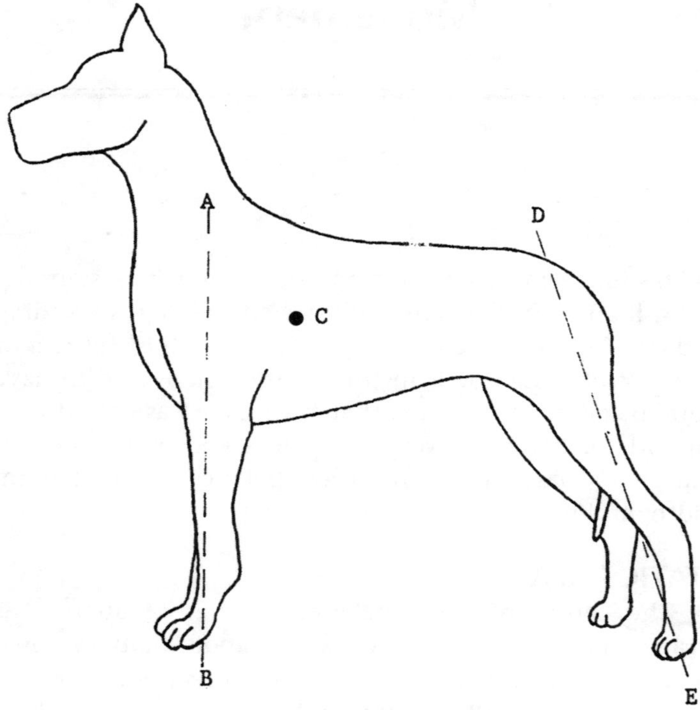

Static Balance Profile of the Dog

1. *AB—line through the center of static balance of the front of the dog.*
2. *C—center of gravity.*
3. *DE—line through the center of static balance of the rear of the dog.*

the center line of the dog. These dogs will have broader chests and be much more heavily muscled as a result. These extra muscles will be required if the dog is to have sufficient tension to hold and move the front legs in accordance with the description in the standard. The Bulldog is, of course, the most exaggerated example of this condition. In breeds with broad chests and very short legs,

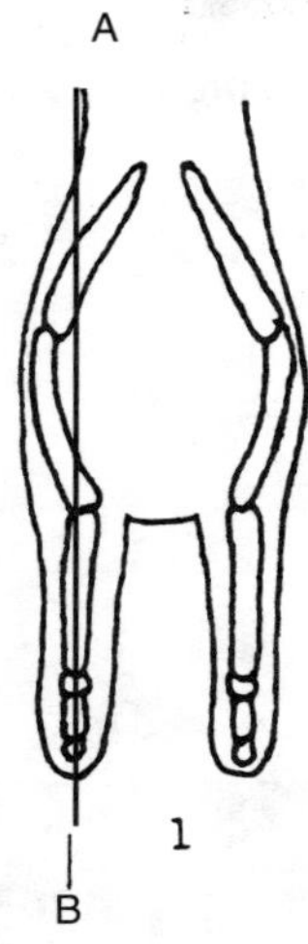

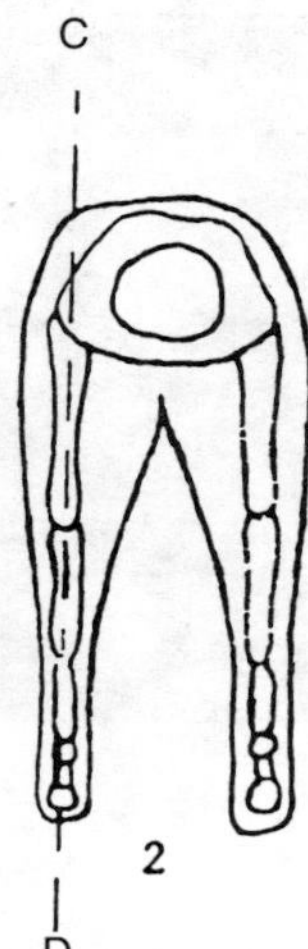

Static Balance Front and Rear Views of the Dog

1. *Front center of balance line AB passes through a column of bone from the scapula to the paw.*
2. *Rear center of balance line CD passses through a column of bone from the pelvis to the paw.*

as in the Basset Hound, the static line of balance will pass through the radius and ulna of the lower leg. This results from the inward curve of these bones as they wrap around the rib cage.

When viewed from the side, the static line of balance of the forequarters will pass from the center of balance of the scapula down a line that will be perpendicular to the ground. This line will pass through the front portion of the fore leg and through the heel of the pad of the front foot. The exact part of the front leg through which this line passes depends on the angle of the shoulders and the slant of the front pasterns. Ideally the line would have bone support as well as that of the pad. Weak pasterns put

Dog in profile show pose to demonstrate static balance.

Same dog gaiting to demonstrate contrast with kinetic balance.

Front of dog in show pose to demonstrate static balance.

undue stress on the forequarters, for they put an unnatural amount of stress on the muscles rather than on the column of bone support.

As man has tampered with the natural process of selection and has created new breeds, he has so changed the anatomy of dogs that the dog does not always achieve both static and kinetic balances that are consistent with each other. One is at times sacrificed to the other to achieve the desired aesthetic effect in the breed.

The static balance of the hindquarters of the dog is more affected by these man-made modifications. It is seen in numerous breeds where the length of the rear legs has been increased to the detriment of the static balance. A number of breed standards call for the angulated hindquarters. The line between well angulated and overly angulated rears has been consistently passed in a number of specimens seen in the ring today.

When seen from side, the ideal static balance for the hindquarters of a dog would have the static line of balance pass from the rear of the buttocks down the front of the rear pastern and be perpendicular to the ground. This would give the greatest line of support for the rear of the dog. Viewed from the rear a line would drop from the ball and socket joint of the hip and pass down the inside of the femur, the tibia, the fibula and the inside of the rear pastern. This would provide a base sufficiently wide to support the weight of the hindquarters.

In some breeds the distance between the static line of balance and the front of the rear pastern is greatly increased. In many cases this increase in angulation of the rear has not been matched by the increased angulation of the forequarters which causes the dog to have a poor gait. A dog that is overly angulated in the rear puts additional stress on the muscles of the back. Depending on the degree of overangulation, the topline will either sag or have an extra buildup of muscles. Either of these

Rear of dog in show pose to demonstrate static balance.

two conditions would not be correct but merely compensatory to the problem. Examples of this condition can be seen in the Doberman Pinscher and in the Setters, among other breeds.

When an exhibitor tries to set a dog up in a show pose that overextends his static balance, the dog will move one or more feet to maintain this balance. One of the failings of novice exhibitors is to stretch the dog too far and put him in an unnatural pose considering his angulation. The novice fails to understand what the dog is trying to communicate and will reset the moved leg several times. This will go on until either the dog gives up and decides he will just not be able to stand in a relaxed position or the exhibitor gives up in exasperation. Experienced exhibitors fully understand the physical limitations of the dog they are exhibiting and have trained their dog to pose in optimum position considering these physical limitations. The exhibitor who fails to understand thoroughly these limitation usually succeeds in exaggerating the faults rather than in minimizing them. The prime responsibility of the exhibitor is to minimize the dog's faults and accentuate his strengths. Unfortunately, the novice usually does just the opposite and makes all ringside aware of his dog's shortcomings.

KINETIC BALANCE

Static balance deals with the dog at rest. All forces are in balance and the dog can relax without the necessity of moving any part of his body to achieve this balance. As soon as the dog starts to move, these forces all change and the dog must now achieve kinetic balance so that he will

Same dog gaiting to demonstrate contrast with kinetic balance.

not fall. Kinetic balance is then the ideal balance between the various forces exerted on a dog when he is gaiting. The speed at which the dog moves modifies the balance needs and, therefore, changes the kinetic lines of balance. When the dog walks very slowly, the front and rear lines of static balance are little changed, but as the dog moves through the trot and into the gallop the lines begin to converge at their farthest point away from the body. The feet tend to move toward each other with the increase in speed. In some breeds the forward line of motion of the right side and the left side approach each other until they blend into a single line and the dog is truly single tracking. Some standards call for single tracking while other standards say that the dog tends to single track as speeds increase. Still other standards state that the legs move straight forward which means that the legs move in parallel planes and that they are the same distance apart no matter at what speed the dog is moving. Many judges do not believe that moving forward in a straight line and moving parallel are the same thing. Moving forward in a straight line is interpreted to mean that the dog does not crab. It is, therefore, not the same thing as moving with the legs parallel to each other.

Moving with the legs parallel is not a natural condition for an animal. No animals in the wild move in this fashion as it is a slow gait that cannot be maintained for any length of time. Even animals as broad as the elephant tend to single track. Parallel movement results at times when there is an imbalance in the lengths of the scapula and the humerus. If the angle of the joint between these two bones is wide and the humerus is short, the dog will have a stilted movement and his front legs may well move parallel to each other. The gait will be very stiff and exaggerated and not pleasing to watch. Both Fox Terrier standards call for the forelegs to hang perpendicular and swing parallel with the sides of the dogs.

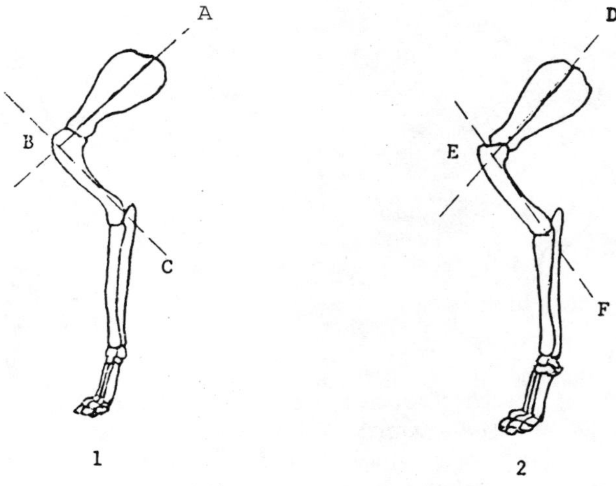

Skeletal Structure of the Forequarters

1. *The angle of the forequarters A-B-C at the point of shoulder is approximately 90 degrees, which is described as ideal in many breeds.*
2. *The angle of the forequarters D-E-F at the point of shoulder is approximately 100 degrees, which is common in many dogs. As the angle increases, the dog becomes more straight in front.*

An interesting experiment can be performed by the reader. If he will mark two parallel chalk lines the same distance apart as are his feet when he is standing relaxed and comfortable and then try to walk along these lines he will discover the unnaturalness of this concept of gaiting with the legs parallel. To appreciate the extreme of this condition, the reader should then try to trot and run down these same lines. It is nearly impossible for any distance and is a slow process. It is very tiring and puts added stress on the muscles of the legs and the back.

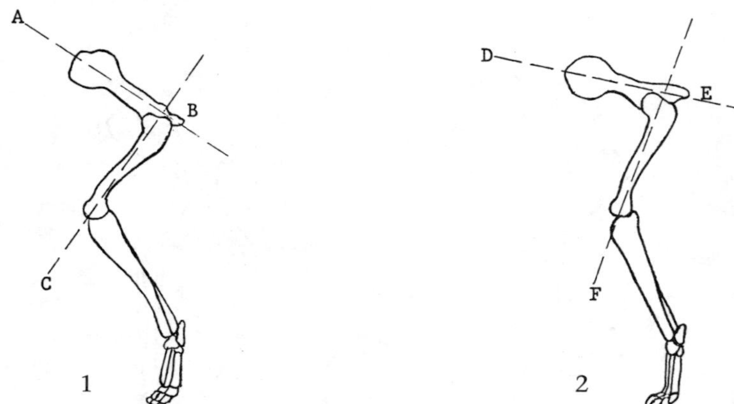

Skeletal Structure of the Hindquarters

1. *The angle of the hindquarters A-B-C is 90 degrees. The croup is at an angle of 45 degrees and would be considered steep.*
2. *The angle of the hindquarters D-E-F is about 80 degrees, which makes the dog straight in rear. The croup is at an angle of 30 degrees, which is considered ideal in many breeds.*

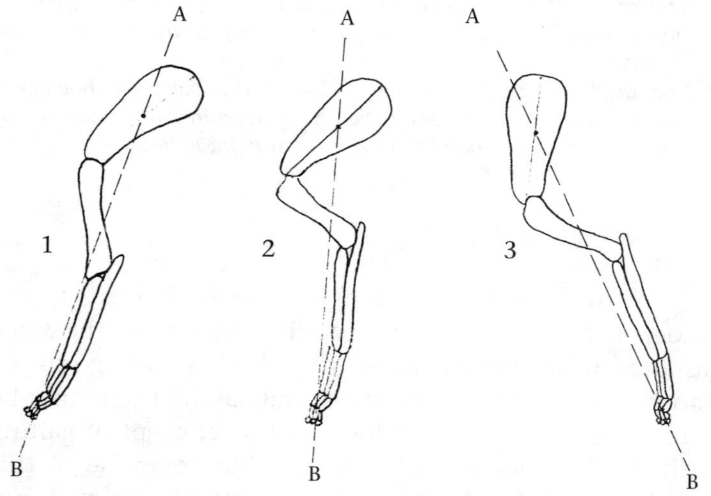

Skeletal Structure of the Forequarters in Motion

The line A-B passes through the center of balance, which is the midpoint of the scapula and the paw. 1. Forward reach. 2. Directly under the body of the dog. 3. Rear extension.

GAIT

The gait of the dog should be clearly defined by the standard for the breed. This unfortunately is not always true as many standards fail to discuss the proper gait for that breed. When this is the case the judge must use his general knowledge of that breed to determine the correct gait when taking into account the physical characteristics of the breed.

The speed at which a dog moves will affect those factors which comprise the elements of gait. The speed will affect the length of stride, the reach, the timing of the foot falls, and even the sequence of the moving of the legs. Closely related to the sequence of the leg movement is the number of feet which are or which are not in contact with the ground at any given moment. The dog moving at a slow pace will have three feet on the ground and one in suspension and moving. The amble is a slightly faster gait than the walk. In this gait the second foot lifts just a fraction of a second before the first foot makes contact with the ground. In the trot the diagonal feet will be in contact with the ground and the two other diagonal feet will be moving. The pace is another two-beat gait but is a much slower gait and is more closely related to the walk or amble in speed. When pacing, the dog moves the two feet on one side at the same time. It is a more relaxed and less tiring gait. The gallop is a four-beat gait in that the dog maintains contact with the ground with only one foot at a time. The double suspension gallop is also a four-beat gait but is much faster than the gallop. It is also characterized by the fact that twice during each sequence no foot is in contact with the ground and the body of the dog is in complete suspension. The first time is when the front legs are fully extended forward and the rear legs fully extended backward. The second time is when all legs are fully contracted toward the center with the front legs passing the rear legs.

A line drawing of a Pembroke Welsh Corgi showing ideal forward reach and rear drive. The bone and muscle structure of the dog determines his ability to move—not his size.

Gait, of course, depends on the flexion and extension of the legs, but other factors must also be taken into consideration to fully understand the mechanics of gait. The back and loins of the dog play an important role in giving the dog the maximum range in both flexion and extension. Coursing hounds have a muscled arch over the loins which strengthens the back and allows it to have the necessary flexion to enable the dog to achieve high speeds when galloping. As the weight of the head and the length of the neck modify the location of the center of gravity and move the center forward, it is imperative that these two elements be correct and in balance with the size and weight of the dog if he is to move efficiently. The distance between the withers allows the dog to lower its head when racing or restricts it from doing this. The tail is also a factor to be considered in the gait of the dog. While it does not add to or detract from the speed for many dogs, it does serve as a rudder and helps the dog maintain his balance. The tail is of great importance in the herding breeds,

This is a series of four photographs of sound Labrador Retriever "A" that moves smoothly with good reach and drive. The left front leg begins the forward stroke with the paw just lifting off the ground.

The paw is lifted higher in order to reach forward.

The forearm has passed the forward part of the chest.

As speed picks up, the paw is lifted.

At full speed, the foreleg reaches its full forward extension.

This is a series of four photographs of Labrador Retriever "B." This dog is sound but has different angulation. The dog is balanced between the front and rear, but both shoulders and hips are slightly more straight.

The wrist is directly below the point of shoulder as the leg moves forward.

It is evident from these two photos that Labrador Retriever "B" does not have the same angulation as does Labrador Retriever "A" (previous page).

especially those which have short backs and must make tight turns when herding farm animals. A tail that is placed too high or too low will be inefficient and not allow the dog full flexibility.

The forequarters of the dog provide the reach while the hindquarters provide the drive. When the dog is in balance and the forces exerted by reach and drive are equal, the dog will have correct movement. His gait will be free and easy and will not be tiring. When these factors are not in correct balance, the gait will be strained and will produce stress on the muscle system of the dog. This stress will result in compensation on the part of the dog and he will consciously do something to alter this stress-producing situation. One of the most common compensating actions of a dog to relieve an uncomfortable condition is to crab or sidewind. Another action could be padding or overextending the front legs to achieve the same goal that can be attained by crabbing. The dog may slow his timing or he may break stride when he is physically unable to maintain a certain gait that has been arbitrarily set by the exhibitor.

FOREQUARTERS

The bones of the forequarters from top to bottom are the scapula, the humerus, the radius and ulna, the carpals, the metacarpals, and the phalanges. These bones give shape to the forequarters and serve as the column of support for the front of the dog. For the bones to serve the dog fully they must be bound together with flexible muscles. The muscles give support to the bones and allow them to move. Each bone is served by opposing and compensating pairs of muscles. One of these muscles will contract and pull the bone in the direction of the contraction. The opposing muscle will relax at the same time and allow the bone to pull toward the contracting muscle. A bone can be served by more than one pair of muscles. Long bones will

Forward Movement
The line of movement is toward the left just as the judge would see the dog move in the ring.

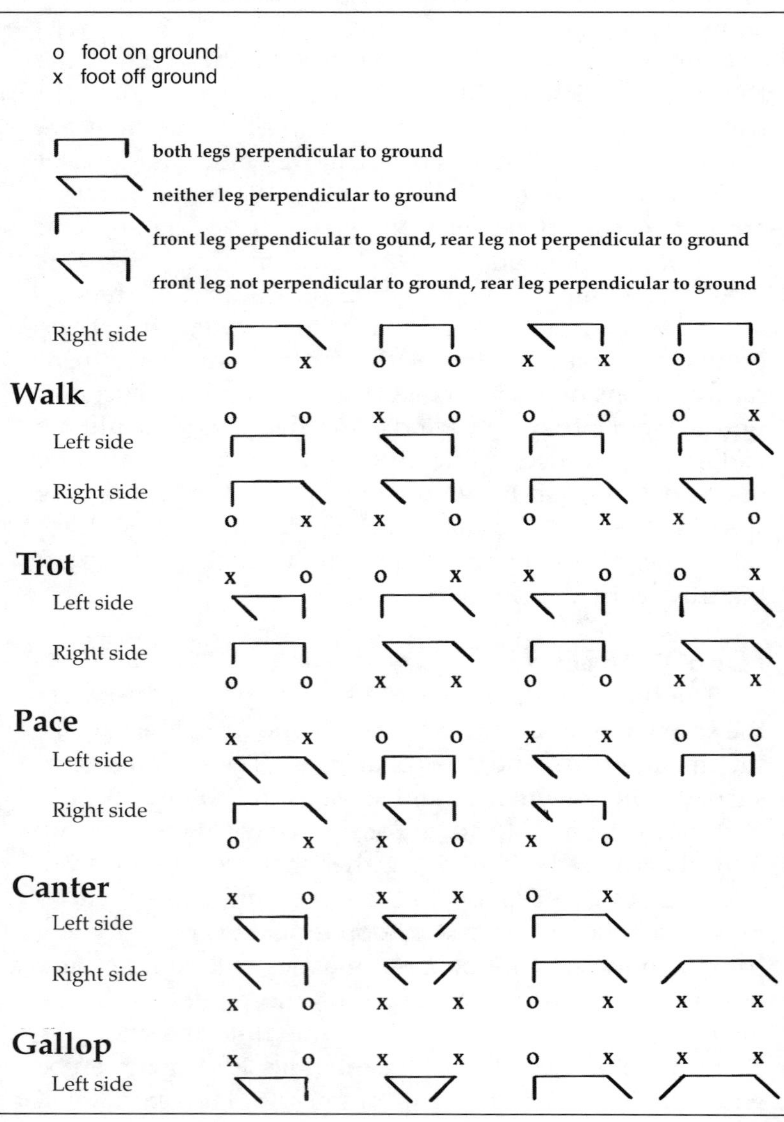

have muscles both at the top and at the bottom. These additional muscles must be coordinated with all others attached to the same bone or there would be little or no movement at all.

The top edges of the scapulae form the withers. The distance between the withers may be small or large depending on the purpose for which the dog was bred. The scent hounds who must get their noses on the ground to follow a trail need sufficient distance between the withers to allow the neck freedom of movement. The distance between the withers of the sight hounds is proportionately less as they hold their heads high when they are coursing game. These dogs do not need to put their noses to the ground when gaiting.

The scapula is attached to the spine by the two opposing trapezius muscles. The trapezius muscle is a sheet-like element which is attached from the top portion of the cervical spine down to the withers. The sheet then extends in triangular fashion halfway down the front side of the central spine or ridge of the scapula. The rear trapezius muscle runs down the thoracic spine from the withers to the sixth or seventh thoracic vertebrae. It stretches forward and down to join to the rear side of the spine of the scapula. It is only attached to about the top third of the scapula.

The rhomboideus muscle is much stronger than the trapezius muscle and is located under the trapezius. These muscles work in tandem. On the underside of the scapula itself are the serratus ventralis muscles. These muscles help in the rotation of the scapula around the center of balance point which is located at midpoint on the spine of the scapula. The serratus ventralis muscles also help determine the distance between the withers. When these muscles are overly developed they become thick and in so doing increase the distance between the tips of the scapulae. Since the center of balance point is located midway

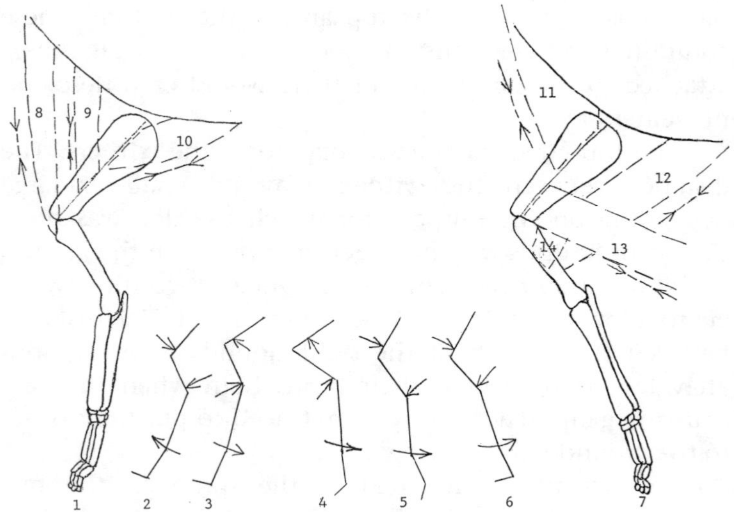

Position changes of bone and muscle of the forequarters as the dog moves forward.

1. Leg ready to move forward.
2. Leg lifts forward. Arrow shows direction bones move as muscles contract and relax.
3, 4, 5, 6. Leg moves to full rear extension.
7. Leg fully extended to the rear.
8. Brachiocephalicus.
9. Serratus.
10. Trapezius.
These muscles contract to pivot around the center point of balance to move the lower end of the scapula forward and allow the leg to reach forward.
11. Trapezius.
12. Levator humeri.
13. Pectoralus profundus.
14. Dorsal.
These muscles contract to pivot around the center point of balance to move the lower end of the scapula rearward to allow the leg to extend rearward.

down the scapula, the bone has only to rotate around this point. If this point were at the tip of the scapula, the base of this bone would have to move in a wide arc which would weaken its stability and require exaggerated extension and flexion of the shoulder muscles. This is just one of the many examples of efficiency of design found in the dog.

The humerus is tied to the scapula by the deltoideus muscles superficially and more deeply by the biceps and the brachialis. By alternately contracting and relaxing, these muscles allow the humerus to move forward and backward, opening and closing the angle of the shoulder joint formed between the scapula and the humerus. This action allows the dog to reach the leg forward and to gait. The triceps are very strong surface muscles that also function in the movement of the humerus as they run from the scapula to the radius and ulna of the lower leg and help in working the scapula-humerus joint.

The lower leg, consisting of the radius and ulna bones, is attached to the humerus by the extensor carpi radialis in the front and by the extensor carpi ulnaris in the rear. These muscles open and close the elbow joint between the humerus and the radius and ulna. Because of the greater length of the lower leg, the arc it can achieve is much greater than that of the humerus.

The lateral digital extensors joining the radius and ulna to the carpi permit the movement of the pastern. These muscles allow the dog to flex the pastern joint sufficiently to get the paw out of the way as the dog arcs his leg forward. If there is not sufficient flexion in this joint, the dog will have an exaggerated front action. He will have to spring with each step in order to avoid striking the ground with the tip of the paw as it makes its forward swing. This is one of the causes of the bouncing topline of a dog. This is not a common problem, but is one element that must be weighed when analyzing a faulty topline during gaiting.

HINDQUARTERS

The middle gluteal muscles connect the femur to the lumbar spinal column while the superficial gluteal muscles connect the femur to the pelvis. These two sets of muscles give stability to the femurs and consequently to the rear of the dog. The tensor fascia lata connects the lumbar spine to the front side of the femur and by contracting permits the tibia to move forward.

The cranial sartorius connects the front of the pelvis to the tibia and fibula across the hip joint formed between the pelvis and the femur and gives additional strength in the closing of this joint. The semitendinosus connects the rear of the pelvis to the tibia and fibula across the femur,

Position changes of bone and muscle of the hindquarters as the dog moves forward.

1. Leg moving forward. 2. Leg lifts forward. Arrows show direction bones move and muscles contract and relax. 3, 4, 5, 6. Leg moves to full rear extension. 7. Leg fully extended to the rear. 8. Caudal sartorius. 9. Fascia lata. 10. Anterior digital extensor. These muscles contract to lift the leg forward. 11. Cranial sartorius. 12. Gastrocnemius. These muscles relax to allow the leg to extend to the rear.

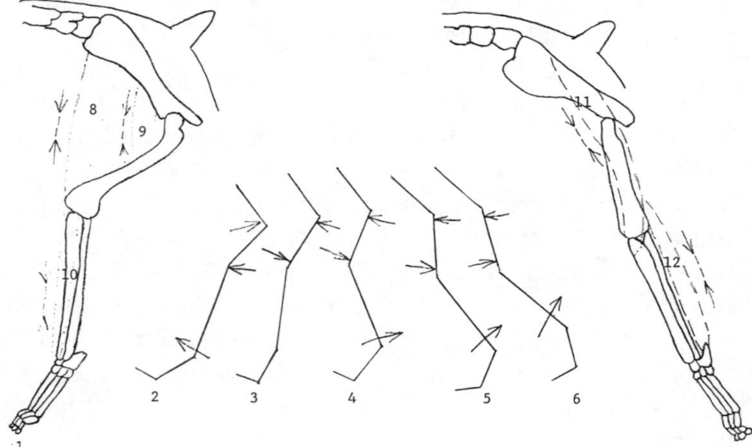

The male handler allows the dog to move with his head down in a more natural position for gaiting.

(Left and Below): These two pictures demonstrate the effect that different handling techniques have on the gait of a dog. Both pictures are of Labrador Retriever "A" with the correct angulation.

Not allowing the dog to gain full advantage of the angulation will seriously affect both reach and drive as the freedom of movement is being severely restricted.

The female handler (right) holds the dog's head higher than the male handler (above), which pulls the dog up and does not let him get the full advantage of the angulation.

adding additional strength. The biceps femoris extends the length of the femur from the pelvis to the top half of the tibia. This sheet-like muscle supplies the shape and bulk to the rear of the upper thigh and the side and back of the lower thigh.

The tendon of gastrocnemius, the superficial digital flexor, the deep digital flexor and the anterior digital flexor supply the muscle power for the rear pastern in both flexion and extension. These muscles allow the dog to retract the foot sufficiently so that it will not come in contact with the ground as the rear leg moves through the arc from complete rear extension to complete forward reach.

PROBLEMS IN GAITING

A dog that has correct angulation both front and rear is said to be balanced. A dog that is balanced in angulation may still have a problem in gaiting if the muscles are not in balance as well. A dog may be overloaded in shoulders and have the correct muscle proportions in the rear. Or he may be just the opposite with the front's being correct and the rear's being overly muscled. Either of these muscle imbalances will be reflected in the gait of the dog.

When the dog is balanced in both angulation and muscles, he should have a smooth and flowing gait. It is assumed that in those breeds that do not discuss the gait, the dog will move straight forward with the limbs swinging freely. As speed increases, the paws will tend to converge toward the center line of forward motion. There will be no restriction in the movement of the legs and the dog will move freely and smoothly with a topline that does not bounce up and down. Those breeds which require a particular gait will define that gait in their standards. Examples of special gait are found in the Bulldog, the German Shepherd, and the Welsh Corgi to mention just three.

PROBLEMS OF FRONT-REAR BALANCE

Overreaching is a condition found in many dogs and occurs when there is not correct balance between the angulation of the forequarters and the angulation of the hindquarters of the dog. The rear is over-angulated in comparison to the front, resulting in the rear's reaching beyond the rearmost placement of the front feet. A dog can take a number of different actions to avoid stepping on his own front feet.

Pounding is the most serious result of overreaching and is caused by an imbalance between the reach of the front legs and the drive of the rear legs. In this condition the front legs do not reach the optimum stride and they are forced to strike the ground before the drive of the rear legs has been expended. This forces the front feet to strike the ground extremely hard, putting stress on the muscles, and results in a braking action during forward motion. This is a very serious fault, for it causes great physical stress to the shoulders as the striking force is transferred directly up the column of bones. There is little flexion of the front leg joints at this time to help absorb this direct shock.

Padding is a suspended action movement of the front legs on the part of the dog to avoid pounding. When the front is straighter than the rear and the forequarters are forced to overreach, the dog lifts the front feet higher than normal to delay the striking of the foot on the ground until the forward motion has been neutralized. This lowers the stress on the forequarters but is not an efficient movement.

Paddling is another inefficient gait. In this case the pad and the pastern make a circular or rotating motion with each step. It is not only not pleasant to watch but it also prevents the dog from maintaining a sustained gait over a given period of time. When the foot strikes the ground, it is coming down with a circular motion rather than one going in the same direction of the forward movement of the dog. This fault does not distribute the shock of the pad hitting the ground in the most effective and stress relieving action for the dog.

Winging is related to paddling but instead of the foot's moving in a circular pattern the paw flips to the outside. While this motion may be more efficient than paddling because the foot strikes the ground in line with the forward line of motion, it is not as effective as the straight back and forward movement of the pastern.

Hackney gait, if a fault, is also the result of an imbalance between the front and rear quarters. Instead of moving the rear sideways in an effort to avoid stepping on his own front feet, the dog lifts the front feet high and thus changes the timing sequence to avoid the problem. This is a result of overreaching with the rear. In the Miniature Pinscher this action is not a fault and is more the result of a difference in the ratio of the lengths of the scapula and the humerus. The shorter humerus with the resulting wider angle at the point of shoulders causes the dog to lift the front feet unnaturally high.

Crabbing or *sidewinding* is a fault of forward movement. To avoid problems in overreaching, the hindquarters angle slightly off the parallel of the center line of forward motion. This center line of forward motion should be directly below the spinal column and will be exactly in this position if the dog has correct balance. As the dog moves his rear slightly to the side, he angles the spinal column away from the center line of forward motion. This causes the dog to gait at an angle and while it causes a degree of stress, it is less serious than pounding. This is the least serious of the faults related to overreaching. While it is the least serious, it is certainly not aesthetically pleasing.

Pacing is a two-beat gait. It is essentially that of the two legs on the same side of the body moving together at approximately the same time. This tends to make the dog sway slightly from side to side. In a square dog like the

Old English Sheepdog, this is a correct gait. By pacing, the square dog can avoid crabbing if the rear is overly angulated. In almost all other dogs this gait is considered a minor fault. In many dogs this gait is used to relieve fatigue after strenuous exercise. All of the larger game animals use this gait almost exclusively while moving slowly. Pacing is the least serious of all the gaiting faults. This is because it is a relief gait and puts the least amount of stress on the muscles and tendons.

PROBLEMS OF THE FOREQUARTERS

Straight shoulders is one of the causes of the imbalance between the forequarters and the hindquarters. There are in addition other problems associated with the forequarters. These can involve the elbows and the carpals or the pastern.

Weaving results from incorrect elbow structure. The musculature at the elbows is not strong enough to hold the elbows in the correct position and as a result the elbow twists, permitting the front feet to cross. To compensate for this the dog usually will toe out.

Toeing out can be a condition of both the front feet and the rear feet. In the front it is the result of the dog's being too close at the carpal joint and the feet turn out to increase the base and give the dog greater stability. In either case it means that the feet do not point directly forward in the direction of the line of movement.

Out at elbows results in sloppy front movement. The elbows do not conform to the natural line of the leg below the point of shoulder. The elbows stand out from this line and therefore cause a loose movement. This is caused by too round a rib cage or weak muscles and results in muscle strain.

Tied at elbows is the opposite of being out at elbows. Because the dog cannot swing the front legs freely forward, he tends to swing the feet farther out than he would normally do. This moves the striking point for the front foot wide of where it should be in order to give greater stability. This fault causes the dog to paddle.

Broken pasterns result from a problem in the carpals. Whatever the cause of this condition, the result is that the slope of the pastern is too great and that the striking force of the paw against the ground cannot be evenly distributed. This puts great stress on the muscles of the shoulders and as a result tires the dog.

Running downhill refers to the condition of a dog's being lower at the withers than he is at the highest point of the croup. This causes the front paw to receive the force of landing on the rearmost part of the paw and does not distribute the force correctly up the leg.

PROBLEMS OF THE HINDQUARTERS

Problems of the hindquarters can result from the overall angulation of the dog, the stifle joint, the hock joint, or the pastern. Problems of the rear are usually less stressful on the dog because the rear does not support the same proportion of the weight as does the front. The forequarters carry 65% to 75% of the weight and therefore faults involving the front are more serious.

Crossing can involve both the forequarters and the hindquarters of the dog. In order to avoid interference from each other, the rear feet swing in an arc around each other. This results in one foot crossing over the direct line of motion of the other foot. This causes the rear to sway from side to side. It is an inefficient gait.

Pitching is a rotating motion of the rear legs. The leg is not stable in its forward rotation and the paw makes a circular pattern before striking the ground. This puts stress on the muscles. While the condition is principally in the rear it can influence the movement of the forequarters as well.

Moving close with stifles out causes the pasterns to move too close to each other for an efficient gait. This is called moving close. This condition sometimes forces the dog to increase the distance between the stifles. This is a bowlegged movement and puts stress on the muscles and ligaments.

Moving close with stifles tied is also called brushing because the pasterns may touch each other during gaiting. If the stifles are tied the rear can be unusually narrow and the one leg may be too close to the other leg. This condition does not provide sufficient drive.

PROBLEMS OF THE HOCKS

Problems in the area of the hocks have a direct effect on the drive of the rear quarters. The degree of the deviation from what is normal determines the seriousness of the fault.

Sickle hocks is a condition in which the hocks are not perpendicular to the ground. The feet are forward of the normal position. This results in a weakened rear and does not provide the necessary drive for the forward motion. It causes the topline to bounce and provides only inefficient movement.

Cow hocks is the condition in which the hocks point toward each other rather than straight to the rear. This forces the feet to point outward rather than straight forward in the line of forward motion. This results in muscular stress and would decrease the drive of the rear.

Spread hocks is the condition in which the hocks point outward which will cause the toes to point inward. It is the opposite of being cow hocked. This condition cannot provide sufficient rear drive.

Twisting hocks results from weak muscles and tendons at the hock joint. As the foot strikes the ground and the weight is beginning to be received on the foot, the hock will weave both in and out in an unstable fashion. This dog will have poor rear drive.

Snatching hocks is the condition in which the hock is pulled abruptly outward as it passes the other leg when moving forward. It is an inefficient movement and does not give strong support to the rear and results in a swaying rear movement.

Toeing in is just the opposite of toeing out. A dog will tend to toe in if he is too wide in front or is out at elbows. In the rear he will toe in if he has spread hocks.

EVALUATING GAITING FAULTS

Gaiting faults involving the forequarters are more serious than those of the hindquarters. This is because of the distribution of weight and the fact that the center of gravity of the dog is located just behind the front legs. However, depending on the fault, a minor degree of fault in the front could well be assigned less significance than a major fault of the rear. With everything being equal, which it never is, pounding is the most serious fault and pacing is the least serious because one is extremely stressful and tiring and the other is frequently a gait used to alleviate stress.

The rest of the faults fall somewhere in between these two. Those involving joints and their supporting muscles are serious because they cause stress and this tires the dog and causes the condition to get progressively worse. Problems involving angulation and the ratio between adjoining bones, while they can cause non-natural gaiting, are usually less stressful on the dog. The degree of the seriousness of the fault is in direct proportion to the degree of stress it causes the dog.

Self-Test Questions

1. What is static balance?
2. What is kinetic balance?
3. What is the pace?
4. What elements move the center of gravity forward from midbody?
5. The static line of balance passes through what part of the scapula?
6. When one of the paired muscles contracts, what does the other one do?
7. What is the most serious gaiting problem?
8. What is the least serious gaiting problem?
9. What is the term used to describe the gait when the feet cross each other?
10. What is the term used to describe the exaggerated high-stepping gait of the front legs?
11. What is another term for crabbing?
12. What is the term used to describe hocks that do not have rear extension?

Self-Test Questions

13. When does parallel movement sometimes result?
14. How does the speed at which a dog moves affect gait?
15. What do the forequarters of a dog provide regarding movement?
16. What do the hindquarters of a dog provide regarding movement?
17. What is the prime responsibility of the exhibitor when showing a dog?
18. What are the bones of the forequarters?
19. What function do the middle gluteal and superficial gluteal muscles serve?
20. What are three breeds that require a special gait?
21. What is "winging"?
22. What are five problems of the forequarters?
23. What are six problems of the hocks?
24. Why are gaiting faults involving the forequarters more serious than those involving the hindquarters?

Breed Type

Identifying breed type is to identify those qualities in a particular dog that will define its characteristics and allow it to be categorized under a specific breed. The ability to do this is a basic requirement of both the exhibitor and the handler as well as the judge. The judge, for example, must have a thorough understanding of those individual qualities that distinguish a Welsh Terrier from a Lakeland Terrier if he hopes to judge these two breeds. If these individuals do not have a command of this information, they are most certainly dealing with a breed in which they do not have competence.

When a judge looks at a Lhasa Apso, a Tibetan Terrier, or a Shih Tzu, he must readily be able to identify the breed if he expects to judge it. For individuals experienced in these three breeds this should present no problem, but for the casual ringside observer it is frequently a different situation. Comments from such observers usually indicate that they can see little or no difference between these breeds and do not understand how anyone can distinguish between them. If these individuals were to study the standards and examine specific dogs they would undoubtedly begin to have an appreciation for these breeds.

It is assumed that exhibitors have a substantial working knowledge of the breed they are exhibiting, but this is not always true. An exhibitor occasionally asks a question which indicates that he has either not read the standard or has not understood it. Most exhibitors are knowledgeable

An appreciation for type results from careful study of breed characteristics. This head study is of Ch. Caimar Cat Dancer, owned by Don and Nancy Petrulis.

about disqualifications but somewhat less familiar with the faults listed in the standards. They do not always remember proportions and ratios or shapes and sizes. An exhibitor who shows several breeds occasionally quotes something from a standard, but has assigned the statement to the wrong breed and appears to be amazed when this is pointed out to him.

No matter what the mastery of the exhibitor is in regards to the standard, the judge must have a complete command of the material and he will have if he is competent and conscientious. He must know the standard and must be able to explain and interpret it when the occasion arises. If he has this knowledge he will not feel intimidated or insecure no matter what the attitude of the exhibitor might be.

While all standards should define type in their description of the breed, some, however, do a much better job than others. Some standards are extremely specific and describe in great length individual characteristics of the breed, while other standards are quite vague and do not even mention certain parts of the dog. A number of standards do not discuss the gait for the breed which allows each individual to define the dog's gait for himself. This is not a good situation in any breed. All physical elements of the dog should be defined by the standard so that all those involved with the breed are working from a common ground.

When a judge looks at a specific dog, he should be able to explain those qualities that set this breed of dog apart from all other breeds. To do this he needs to know the general outline of the dog which reflects the height and weight ratio. The dog may be tall or short, may have a heavy frame or be light-boned. Whatever these qualities are in this dog, they should match what the standard says they are to be.

After looking at the overall picture of the dog, the judge then looks at the various parts to make certain that these parts represent what they should for this breed. The length, width, and shape of the head must match its description. The length and substance of the neck must be in balance with the head as well as the trunk of the dog. The torso has to be correct for the breed and in balance with the head and neck. The forequarters and the hindquarters must be in proportion and have the proper angulation as defined by the standard. Whether the coat is long or short, smooth or rough, trimmed or natural, curly or straight depends on the requirements of the breed. In addition to these qualities, the dog must gait in the correct manner as defined by the needs of the breed as this is also a part of the type of a breed.

In evaluating the dog, the judge must remember and take into account the history of the breed. This would include the original purpose for the creation of the breed that set him apart from other breeds already in existence. While not many dogs continue to serve the purpose for which they were originally bred, a number still do. Many of the Sporting dogs are still used in the field for hunting as are certain of the Hounds. Herding dogs frequently still serve as herding animals and Working dogs are still used as guard dogs. Not many Terriers continue to be used for hunting rodents and other small game, even though their histories frequently deal with this aspect of their development. Toy dogs were bred to be companions and they most certainly continue to serve man in this area. Non-Sporting dogs, with the exception of the Poodle, are different from the rest of the breeds. Their common denominator is difficult to define. The Poodles were, of course, water retrievers.

Type is then defined as those innate physical qualities which are characteristic to one breed and one breed alone. It is these qualities and their unit balance that are distinct and unique to only that one particular breed. They will not match any other breed. In addition to these static physical characteristics, the judge must also consider the gait of the dog when it moves and must also consider the personality and the temperament of the specific dog being examined. A Toy dog is not expected to act like a Terrier and a Terrier is certainly not expected to act like a Toy. Neither of these conditions would be typical of the breed and therefore the dog would not be of the correct type.

Type has to be the single most important element in judging any breed, for it is precisely this quality that distinguishes one breed from another. A dog may be balanced, sound, and in good condition, but if he does not act nor look like the breed he has little or no merit and would certainly not be included in anyone's breeding program. If a dog is not worthy of being included in a breeding program he has no place in the show ring.

The parts of the dog that must be carefully analyzed in order to determine type are: head, neck, forequarters, body, hindquarters, coat, gait, and temperament. These are always the qualities used in judging a dog, but the judge must pay special attention in his physical examination of the dog to ascertain that these parts of this particular exhibit are correct and reflect the uniqueness of the breed as defined by the standard.

HEAD

To determine the correctness of head type, the judge checks the length and the ratio balance between the muzzle and the skull. This ratio differs greatly from breed to breed. The extremes are seen in the Pekingese that has no measurable muzzle and the Borzoi whose length of muzzle equals its length of back skull. The width of the skull in comparison to its length is also significant. The Borzoi has a skull considerably narrower than its length and the Pekingese has a skull that is wider than its length. The step up in planes or the stop between the muzzle and the skull may be exaggerated as in the Bulldog or minimal as seen in the Collie.

The size, shape, and placement of the ears are important in analyzing the head for they can create an illusion that the head is wider or taller or flatter than it may actually be. Hound ears as in the Beagle are set low while the ears of the Tibetan Spaniel rise above the topline of the skull before they fold down to hang close to the sides of the skull. The cropped ears of the Terriers create an illusion that a dog with uncropped ears just does not have. Observing these same breeds in a show ring in England where cropping is not permitted, one does not always feel that he is looking at the same breed. This is certainly true in the case of the Doberman Pinscher and the Great Dane. Seeing these dogs with large, pendent ears leaves an entirely different impression of the breed. Looking at a breed like the Yorkshire Terrier with a small, naturally erect ear is not the same as looking at the cropped ear of the Miniature Schnauzer.

The shape of the ear is important but so is the size of the ear. A breed like the Yorkshire Terrier or the Pomeranian is to have small, erect ears. When one sees a specimen with tall, wide ears the total picture of the dog is destroyed. He does not look like the same breed since the balance of the head has been modified and the head is not typical of the breed.

Ear placement is also of importance. A Pomeranian whose ears are placed too wide apart appears to have a problem of skull size when this may not be the case at all. If the ears are wide apart there is more skull to be seen, but in balance it may be a correct skull with just faulty ear placement. The ears of the Whippet are soft and flexible, and the dog must show his ears to prove that they have the correct amount of erectile tissue. Many a Whippet has lost a placement because he would not use his ears in the ring. If the ears of the Beagle are set near the edge of the skull, the sorrowful, houndy look is lost. The Irish Setter whose ears are placed higher on the skull than are the ears of the Beagle takes on a houndy look when the ears are placed an inch or lower down the side of the skull.

Ears then must be considered when determining the expression of an exhibit. The ears serve to frame the head so if they are out of proportion, too high or too low, or have too much erectile tissue, they change the typical expression for the breed. When this is the case, the dog is not typey of the breed.

The eyes are a major element of the expression and perhaps the focal point in judging the correctness of expression. The eye must be evaluated on size, shape, color, and placement. Most breeds call for a dark eye. Some standards define dark as almost black while others call for various shades of hazel. Breeds that have blue merle as an accepted color will usually accept a blue eye as correct. A blue eye or eyes is also correct in the Dalmatian. In Mexico, however, the blue eye in the Dalmatian is a disqualification. Red or liver colored dogs will usually have a correspondingly lighter eye and still be correct.

A number of breeds call for black eye rims but will accept light or self-colored eye rims in liver dogs. The black eye rims usually create the illusion that the eye is larger than it actually is. This statement can be verified when one finds a dog that has a black eye rim on one eye and no black rim on the other eye. The eye with the black rim looks larger. The blacker the eye rim the larger the eye appears to be. Since this is the case, the judge must be aware he is considering only the eyeball itself when determining eye size. Partially black eye rims make the eye look less intent and less bright and this must be taken into consideration. When there is a problem with the eye rim, the eye should not be faulted but rather the lack of correct pigmentation should be noted.

The placement of the eyes in the head helps to create the character of the breed. The distance between the eyes changes the intensity of the look. Eyes spaced widely apart give an openness to the face and convey a more calm and open expression. Eyes that are closer together give the impression that the dog may be somewhat more nervous or tense. This may well not be the case at all, but it is an impression that one can receive. Whether the eyes are set high in the face or low also can give the impression that the dog is highly attentive and, therefore, more intelligent, or that he is inattentive and dull. All these impressions are what create the expression of the dog and help to identify breed type.

Eye shape is an important aspect in expression. Eyes are usually described as almond-shaped, round, small, or large. The almond-shaped eye is shaped like the almond nut and is oval shaped, being round at one end and coming to a point at the other end. Many standards classify the almond-shaped eye as the correct type for that breed. The round eye is correct in many of the Oriental breeds like the Pekingese, the Shih Tzu, and the Lhasa Apso. In other breeds a round eye is considered faulty as it changes the expression of the dog.

Some standards state that the eye is to be small. The Toy Manchester Terrier standard calls for a small eye as opposed to the Pekingese standard which accepts the larger eye. The reverse of this would just not be acceptable. No one would want a Toy Manchester Terrier with large eyes nor a Pekingese with small eyes.

The size of the nose leather is another element that must be considered when examining the head. Some breeds call for a large nose leather as in the case of the Bouvier des Flandres. The nose leather of the Affenpinscher is by comparison small. Some breeds have extended nose leathers with the top side extending beyond the base side of the nose. This is the case in the Afghan Hound. In profile it can easily be seen that the nose leather extends forward at the top and then recedes toward the bottom. This type of nose on a Beagle would most certainly be out of place.

Dentition can vary greatly across the various breeds. The scissors bite is the desired bite in most breeds. A number of breeds that accept the scissors will also accept an even bite as well. Breeds like the Bulldog and the Affenpinscher will have an undershot bite and be considered typey. A breed like the Lhasa Apso will accept the undershot bite as well as the even bite. The Tibetan Terrier is unique in that it will allow the scissors bite, an even bite, a reverse scissors bite, and an undershot bite. This has caused problems for the breed since a mouth tending toward being undershot will have a different width-to-length ratio than a mouth that tends toward the scissors bite. By failing to limit the bite, the breed has proven difficult to judge by those who have not had long exposure to the breed. Overshot is not really an acceptable bite. The Whippet standard calls for a disqualification if the overbite is more than one-quarter of an inch. Although the wry mouth is never mentioned as an unacceptable bite, it should be so weighted in the evaluation of the head.

Looking at the dog straight on, it is not always possible to see a problem of the mouth. In profile, however, it is much easier to see a problem. When the judge inspects the mouth he can easily determine the bite and at the same time make note of any missing teeth. Since the Doberman Pinscher and the Rottweiler standards call for a disqualification if the dog has a certain number of missing teeth, counting teeth in these breeds is basic.

NECK

The length and the shape of the neck can enhance the elegance of the dog, or they can detract from it by making the dog look coarse and out of balance. While a short, thick neck in one breed may be correct, it would look out of place on a different breed. A typical Bulldog neck on a Labrador Retriever would destroy the Labrador Retriever breed type as would the reverse of this situation destroy the breed type of the Bulldog.

The Bulldog neck is to be "short, very thick, deep and strong and well arched at the back." The neck of the Labrador Retriever is to be "of medium length, powerful and not throaty." While there is no mention in the Labrador Retriever standard about an arch to the neck, there must be at least a slight one or the dog would not have the muscles necessary to work in the field. An absolutely straight neck would not allow the dog to move the neck freely and lower it sufficiently to retrieve birds in the field.

The standard for the Belgian Malinois describes the neck as "round and rather outstretched, tapered from head to body, well muscled with tight skin." The standards for the Belgian Sheepdog and the Belgian Tervuren use similar descriptions including the word *round.* Most breed standards do not use the term round in describing the neck. The American Water Spaniel is another breed that does call for the round neck.

Neck length is important in analyzing the breed type silhouette of the dog as he is standing in a show pose. Some of the terms used to describe neck length in standards are: short, rather short, comparatively short, moderately short, of medium length, moderately long, fairly long, relatively long, of sufficient length, long enough, good length, rather long, or long. These are thirteen different phrases used to express the length of the dog's neck. In addition, the English Foxhound standard states that the neck must be "not less than 10 inches."

When a judge passes on multiple breeds, he must determine for himself exactly how many different lengths there are. There could be as few as three: short, medium, or long. Two additional lengths could be added, one between short and medium and another between medium and long. The question also arises as to what is the difference between moderately short, comparatively short, and rather short. These terms must also be taken in the context of the breed they are describing. A neck of "good length" in an Afghan Hound is not the same thing as a neck of "good length" in the Basenji. It is a question of proportion and balance.

Different standards also use different terms to describe the arch of the neck. Common words used are: arched, nicely arched, rather arched, slightly arched, moderately arched, and well arched. Giving clear and precise definitions for the three middle expressions would be a somewhat challenging task. These terms are just too imprecise to provide a real consensus and do lead at times to a somewhat heated discussion among breeders.

Another problem that arises in the evaluation of necks is brought about by those standards that do not even mention the neck. Among these are the Weimaraner, the Lhasa Apso, and a number of the Toy breeds, such as the Pekingese and the Pug to mention just two. In these cases the judge must rely on his general study of the history and function of the breed. If form is to follow function then the evaluator should be able to determine what is correct for a given breed. Getting others to agree may be a different problem.

FOREQUARTERS

The forequarters consist of the shoulder, the upper arm, the lower arm, the pasterns, and the feet. The shape, size, and proportions of these various parts must be evaluated to insure that they conform to the standard and that they are correct for the breed. While most breeds prefer for the shoulders to be layed back or well layed back, other standards will accept a more upright shoulder. The layback is the angle that the axis of a long bone, the scapula, makes with a horizontal line. While it is accepted in many breeds that this angle would ideally be 45 degrees, there are many specimens that do not achieve this ideal.

A more realistic angle would probably be 50 degrees or more which would produce an angle of 100 degrees where the scapula meets the humerus. It is difficult to determine the exact angle of this joint, but if one holds the thumb and forefinger at a 90-degree angle and then superimposes this angle along the scapula and the humerus, a more correct impression can be obtained.

A number of factors can alter the angle at the point of shoulder. The one already mentioned problem of angle is perhaps the most common cause of straight shoulders. Another problem frequently seen is the imbalance in the ratio of lengths of the humerus in comparison to the scapula. If the humerus is too short, the lower end of the scapula will be pulled toward the rear of the dog which will cause the angle of the shoulder to open and become greater than the ideal. This will also result in the moving forward of the top of the scapula at the withers. This will move the withers up the neck and make the neck itself appear shorter. This will result in an imbalance in length of neck to both the length of body and the height of the dog. These problems can, therefore, not be considered as isolated elements when analyzing the dog, for one problem will frequently affect another area and modify its overall effect.

When the shoulders are out of balance, the elbows will be affected and their freedom will be restricted. This will cause the dog to move his feet in a non-natural or non-normal fashion. This will not be typical for the breed and the dog will have lost one element of type.

The straightness of the bones of the lower leg must also be considered. It is to be assumed that the radius and the ulna are straight unless otherwise specified. The Dachshund permits these bones to be proportionately short and thus causes them to be curved to conform to the shape of the chest. This same situation exists in the Basset Hound. Legs that were absolutely straight in either of these two breeds would be a fault as they would cause a wobbling gait which would not be typey.

When looking at the Bulldog from the front, it appears as if the bones of the lower leg are curved. In some specimens they are in fact curved, but this is not correct. The apparent curve of the legs is the result of the heavy muscling on upper outside of the lower legs just below the elbow. The bones themselves are perfectly straight, but the added muscle mass at this point gives the illusion that the legs are curved.

The joint between the radius and ulna and the metacarpals determines the slope of the front pasterns. Very few breeds call for upright pasterns since this can easily lead to knuckling over which would be a definite weakness of the leg and would have serious consequences on the sustained gait of the dog.

Pasterns that have a slight slope spare the forequarters from excessive strain for they act as shock absorbers when the dog gaits. This added spring dissipates the force of the shock rather than moving it directly up the leg. If the pasterns are too straight too much of the direct shock is passed directly up the leg, which would tire the dog much sooner than should be expected.

Much is said about the terrier front and how it differs from the fronts of many of the other breeds. The standard for the Smooth Fox Terrier calls for the legs to be "straight with bone strong right down to the feet, showing little or no appearance of ankle in front, and being short and straight in pastern." The Kerry Blue Terrier calls for the pasterns to be "short, straight and hardly noticeable." The pasterns of the Welsh Terrier are to be upright and powerful. This condition in these breeds will affect the gait of the dogs as there will be less spring since the stress will be transmitted directly up the leg. The gait of these long-legged Terriers is different from that of dogs in other groups, and is different from some of the short-legged Terriers.

The structure of the forequarters helps in determining the gait of the dog. The gait of the dog is an important element in determining breed type since the gait of each breed should be unique to that breed and be slightly different from the gait of any other breed. This statement is in fact too great a generalization as there are a number of breeds that developed from the same historical stock and therefore have a great many similarities, gait being one of these. The difference in the movement of Setters, for example, may be merely the result of faulty structure rather than any significant difference in gait. These problems of structure can cause a greater difference in gait within a breed than between two similar breed specimens moving correctly.

BODY

The body of the dog includes the thorax and the abdominal cavity along with the thoracic spine, the lumbar spine, and the pelvis. The length, width, and shape of this combined set of structures determines the type for the breed. The coursing Hounds have narrower chests that are proportionately deeper. The Basset Hound, on the other hand, has a broader chest with a much more substantial body. Speed is not as important for him as is staying power on the trail. The same thing can be said for many of the scent Hounds. Endurance is more important than speed.

A number of standards state that the chest must provide plenty of room for both heart and lungs. This statement does not add much to the description for any breed since each healthy dog has the necessary capaciousness or he would not be healthy. Chests are described as narrow, medium in width or wide depending on the breed. Proportionately the widest chest is that of the Bulldog. The narrowest chests would be in the Hounds such as the Greyhound, the Saluki, and the Afghan Hound. A narrow chest can provide adequate room for both heart and lungs as can a very broad chest.

The ratio of the length of back or thoracic spine to the loin area is important in the analysis of breed type. These two elements make up the length of topline, but the balance between the two is what determines the coupling of the dog. Many of the Herding dogs require short coupling so that they may perform their duties in an efficient and effective manner. Being able to make short turns at relatively high speed is necessary if the dog is to keep the flocks herded in a tight manageable unit. A longer coupling would make for wider turns and cause the dog extra work in keeping the animals together.

The standard for the Cardigan Welsh Corgi describes the body as long but the loin as short. This would enable the dog to make the necessary tight turns, but would also indicate that the back is proportionately longer than it would be in a number of other breeds.

The Skye Terrier is probably the longest dog of any breed considering his height. The standard calls for the back to be long but makes no mention of the loin area. Since there is no reference to the length of loin, most judges assume that this area is of average length. When there is no mention of either long or short, medium is assumed to be the norm.

Many of the sight Hounds have some degree of arch over the loins. This generous supply of muscles provides the dog with the additional flexibility needed when the dog is at a full gallop. He must be able to flex the spine in order to get full forward extension of the rear legs and full rearward retraction of the front legs.

The standard for the Siberian Husky states that "The back is straight and strong, with a level topline from withers to croup." The conclusion is then that this is not a dog designed for speed which would require extra flexibility of loin, but one that must perform his work for long periods of time and requires great endurance. This endurance is precisely what a Siberian Husky would need when pulling a sled over miles of snowy trails. The chest that is deep but not broad is able to provide sufficient lung capacity for this Working breed.

The Norwegian Elkhound is a square dog, being as tall at the withers as he is long from the forechest to the rump. "The body is short and close-coupled with the rib cage accounting for most of its length." This describes a dog that is very short in loin. This standard describes a dog that is a very efficient mover. He is capable of sustained travel over a wide variety of ground surfaces. One only has to study the breed gaiting in the show ring to appreciate the efficiency of the gait of this breed.

The tuck-up or lack of tuck-up of a particular breed is another of the elements of type. The sight Hounds, for the most part, have emphasized tuck-ups as opposed to the Golden Retriever which has very little tuck-up. Being able to travel at high speeds is not a requirement of the Retrievers, but being able to swim while carrying a large bird is. The extra development of abdominal muscles is important for this breed, but would be a hindrance in a Hound that must be able to move at the double suspension gallop. Abdominal fullness would inhibit the efficiency of the Hound.

As with other physical aspects of the body of the dog, the tuck-up ranges from little or none to what might almost be classified as exaggerated. Many of the Working and Herding dogs are only slightly tucked-up in the abdomen. The more streamlined the dog, the greater will be the tuck-up. Speed goes with the exaggerated tuck-up while endurance goes with the minimal tuck-up.

The slope of the croup or the lack thereof defines the rear silhouette of the dog. The standard for the Bouviers des Flandres states that "The horizontal line of the back should mold unnoticeably into the curve of the rump." This means that there is little slope at the croup and that the tail is set on at the level of the back.

The croup of the Portuguese Water Dog is "only slightly inclined" while the croup of the Dachshund is "only slightly sinking." The rear of the Whippet is described as having a "not too accentuated arch beginning over the loin and carrying through over the croup, with the arch being continuous without flatness....A steep or flat croup should be penalized." The Afghan Hound standard calls for the rear to have a "falling away toward the stern, with the hipbones very pronounced." This means that there is a definite downward slope to the croup or the hipbones would not be pronounced. The Manchester Terrier standard also describes a downward slope to the croup when it states "back slightly arched at the loin, and falling again to the tail."

The croup provides the finish for the topline. Whether it is almost level, slightly inclined, or inclined completes the silhouette of the outline. A croup that is either overly exaggerated or less angulated than it should be is not typical of the breed and makes the dog less typey than he should be. The angle of the croup affects the entire rear assembly of the dog. A steep croup shortens the rear angulation.

HINDQUARTERS

The muscular hindquarters of the dog provide the driving force for the gait. Since gait is an important element of breed type, the rear assembly must be correct if the dog is to gait correctly. The hindquarters consist of the femur, the tibia and fibula, the tarsals, the metatarsals, and the phalanges plus the associated muscles. The angle of the pelvis and the slope of the croup must also be considered when analyzing the hindquarters as must the arch or lack of arch over the loins since these elements can affect the reach and drive of the rear.

Rear angulation, while a concern of many breeders and judges, is an area that still appears to be misunderstood.

There are many examples of exaggerated over-angulation seen in the ring today. Some exhibitors feel that this exaggerated angulation means that the rear is very powerful and provides extra drive for the dog. This is usually not the case and in many instances causes the dog to have weak rear drive and to be unbalanced with a front that does not have this excess angulation. When the dog is unbalanced he will not move straight forward but will crab, pound, or pad to avoid the consequences of overreaching. This is not powerful rear drive, but rather poor movement.

Comparing the rear angulation of the Rottweiler with that of the Doberman Pinscher is an exercise in contrasts. In the Rottweiler the front plane of the rear pastern is only slightly removed rearward from a line dropped from the rear of the buttocks to the ground. This same line in the case of the Doberman Pinscher would be at a greater distance from the front of the rear pastern. The natural speed at which these two breeds move is partially due to this difference in the rear angulation.

The Chow Chow and the Bulldog are two examples of breeds that have minimal rear angulation. The stifle joint of the Chow Chow shows little angulation and the hock joint appears almost straight. This would indicate that the weight-bearing line of the hindquarters would be almost directly under the weight mass of the rear. The hocks of the Bulldog are slightly bent, which removes them from being directly under the mass of the rear weight. Both of these instances provide for strong and solid static balance, but will have a considerable effect on the kinetic balance of the dog when he moves.

When a breed has little rear angulation, its static balance is improved, but its kinetic balance is adversely affected. The converse of this is also true. When the dog has more than average rear angulation, his static balance is sacrificed but his kinetic balance is improved. Selective breeding has both caused and maintained these conditions and has eliminated the moderating influence that a natural process of selection would have corrected.

The majority of the standards call for the hocks to be well let down which means that the rear pasterns are to be short. Short pasterns improve rear drive since it is easier to tuck the short pastern under than it is if the pastern is longer. When the pastern is longer, the dog will lift the rear higher so that the pastern will clear the ground as he swings his leg forward. This in turn will cause a slight bounce to the rear and will provide atypical movement.

Many breeds call for the rear pasterns to be straight and parallel while others will allow a slight deviation from the perpendicular. The Bulldog standard allows the hocks to be slightly bent which means that there is a resulting slight slope to the pasterns. In any breed when the slope of the rear pasterns is exaggerated the dog is said to be sickle hocked. A sickle hocked dog is one that does not have good rear drive as he cannot get the pad of the rear foot in its optimum rearward extension. The lack of adequate angulation at the hock joint restricts the complete straightening of the rear leg and therefore limits the rear drive.

While most breed standards permit the removal of dewclaws from the rear legs, the absence of dewclaws can be a disqualification in other breeds. The Briard, for example, is disqualified if he has "less than two dewclaws on each rear leg." The Kerry Blue Terrier, on the other hand, is disqualified if he has "dewclaws on the hind legs." Dewclaws can cause a problem in coated breeds so their removal facilitates the grooming process and prevents their being torn. Dewclaws can also cause problems for water dogs working in the winter as the ice shards can cut the dewclaws and cause injury to the dog. However, when the standard requires that they be present they must be there, for this is an element of type.

TAIL

A key element of breed type is the tail of the dog. The tail finishes the general outline of the dog and completes the entire picture of the breed. Tails vary as to length, size, shape, carriage, furnishings, and placement. Change one or more of these elements and the dog is less than ideal as a representative of the breed.

Tails range from virtually non-existent, as in the Old English Sheepdog and the Pembroke Welsh Corgi, to the Scottish Deerhound and the Irish Wolfhound who have very long tails that reach nearly to the ground. Standards in a number of breeds state that the tail should reach the hock joint. The standard for the Whippet requires that the tail be long enough to reach "the hipbones when drawn through between the hind legs." Many breeds have the docked tail which is only a portion of its original length. The Yorkshire Terrier tail is docked as is the tail of the Doberman Pinscher and a number of the Terrier breeds. Docking the tails and cropping of the ears is not legal in many other countries so the breeds really do look different there. Looking at examples of the breed in their natural state gives a true appreciation of just how important tails and ears are in the establishing of breed type.

Some tails have fine bone as in the case of the Manchester Terrier and the Bedlington Terrier, while others have heavier bone as seen in the Bull Terrier. Tails are generally tapering, being thick at the root and tapering down to a finer tip. Tails usually hang straight down when the dog is standing in a relaxed pose, but will be raised when the dog is gaiting or excited. Many standards state that the tail should not be raised above the level of the topline while others permit the tail to be carried up providing it is not carried forward past the root of the tail itself. Still others call for the tail to be carried up and over the back with the end resting on top of the back or falling to either side.

Some tails are placed high on the rather flat croup as is the case of the Bouvier des Flandres, while others have lower placement and continue in an unbroken line the curve of the arched loin as is seen in the Italian Greyhound. When a tail set is lower than it should be, the problem usually lies in a croup that is too steep and is atypical of the breed. Steep croups in turn affect the angulation of the rear which affects the gait of the dog. Because of this it is impossible to separate faults into completely isolated areas as they are inter-related.

The furnishings of the tail complete the picture. The Labrador Retriever has a special tail coat which is one of the keys to the breed. The tail has a "peculiar 'rounded' appearance which has been described as the 'otter' tail." A dog without this particular tail is lacking in breed type. The tail of the Beagle and a number of scent Hounds is to carry a brush or additional longer hair down the back or the underside of the tail. This gives the impression that the tail is thicker than it is in reality. Without this brush the dog appears to have an atypical rattail.

COAT

Coat is an obvious element of type and one that is readily recognized by ringside spectators. Spectators can appreciate coat pattern, but they cannot evaluate coat texture without feeling the hair itself. Coat type is equally as important as quantity if not more so.

A long, flowing coat, either with or without undercoat, is one type and is correct for many breeds. The short coat, with or without undercoat, is another type and could also be correct in some breeds. A scissored coat is correct in the Kerry Blue Terrier and the Bedlington Terrier but would be incorrect in the case of the Cardigan Welsh Corgi. The Cardigan Welsh Corgis are sometimes scissored to conceal an incorrect fluffy coat. Another type of coat is the broken coat found in many of the Terriers. This is a man-made coat and the techniques used in the stripping of these coats are used to enhance the texture of the hair itself. The stripping process makes the hair come in thicker and more coarse.

The coat pattern of the Afghan Hound is unique to the breed with its saddle of shorter hair down the back. The ridge of the Rhodesian Ridgeback is also a unique coat pattern. This ridge is the result of the hair growing in the opposite direction of the rest of the coat of the back. "The ridge must be regarded as the characteristic feature of the breed," and the lack thereof does disqualify the dog.

A number of breeds grow very long coats which do not require trimming. Many exhibitors believe that the longer the hair the better the quality of the dog. The Cocker Spaniel of today is a far cry from specimens of the past. The Cocker Spaniel Ch. My Own Brucie who went Best in Show at Westminster in the 1940's had almost no coat when compared to the specimens in the ring today. Ch. My Own Brucie could easily have worked in the field without being hampered by his coat. The same thing cannot be said about the Cocker Spaniels in the ring today. Their coat would become hopelessly tangled in the brush.

The standard for the Bearded Collie calls for a medium length coat that "allows plenty of daylight under the body." Coats in this breed appear to be getting longer as there is less and less light under the body. The coats of the Tibetan Terriers have increased greatly in length since the breed was first recognized. This standard states that "an area of light should be seen under the dog." There is little or no light under many of the specials seen in the ring today. Breeds like the Lhasa Apso and the Shih Tzu have floor-length coats before the dog is a year old. Many of these coats continue to grow so their coats are trimmed back to floor length to eliminate the possibility that the dog will trip on his own coat while gaiting.

A water dog like the Labrador Retriever has a double coat as protection against the chill of the water and the winds of the fall hunting season. When a dog does not have the required undercoat, he is said to have an open coat. This is incorrect and causes the outer coat to lie flat against the skin and does not provide the dog with the necessary protection from the elements.

Dogs with double coats usually lose their thick winter undercoat in late spring and their thinner summer undercoat early in the fall. This shedding of undercoat allows a new, healthier coat to come in that is more suited for the temperatures of the season. A number of standards call the reader's attention to the lack of seasonal undercoat and state that the dog should not be penalized for this temporary lack of coat.

Coat color is very important in some breeds, but if it is a color that changes with the age of the dog, it is sometimes difficult to predict if the coat of a nice puppy will change to the correct color as the dog matures. This is especially true in the case of the Yorkshire Terrier as the coats break at different ages in different breeding lines. A clue to the future color of the dog is found in the texture of the coat. If the hair has a fine, silky texture it can be assumed that the coat will break to the correct blue and tan. However, if the hair is thick and soft, the chances are that the coat will tend to the black side and will never fully break to blue nor will the sooty quality of the tan of the head completely clear.

The judging of terrier coats requires special training. When a non-terrier judge first moves into the Terrier breeds he needs to devote special attention to the study of these unusual coats. Terrier coats are generally double. When the undercoat dies, it must be removed to allow the new coat to come in. Since the coat does not all fade at the same time, the groomer must roll the coat to keep it at its prime at all times. This is accomplished with the use of the stripping comb or can be accomplished by hand plucking the dead hair. Clipping or scissoring this coat will not produce the same results as it will soften the coat rather than give it body and make it wiry.

The coat of the Miniature Schnauzer and the Brussels Griffon are stripped in sections which produces hair of different length on the body to reflect how long that particular section of the dog has been stripped. While it is possible to roll the coat of the Brussels Griffon, this usually does not work with the same degree of success in the Miniature Schnauzer because of the variation in the coloration of the individual hairs. The coat can look too mottled at times if it is rolled, so many Miniature Schnauzer breeders strip the dog completely and then show it only while the coat is in prime condition and then strip it again. This gives a rather on-and-off-again career to an individual dog.

The coat of the Wire Fox Terrier can usually be kept in show condition for months at a time by judiciously removing the dead hair and at the same time protecting the new incoming coat. There will be times when it will be in full bloom and other times when it will be less so. The coat of the Cairn Terrier is another coat that, if worked on a daily basis, can keep the dog in the show ring almost continuously.

A number of breeds have short, close coats that require no special attention. These dogs need only regular bathing and brushing to eliminate the dead hair and any possible skin irritants. Trimming of the hair around the toes and sometimes the whiskers will make the dog look neater. However, some breeds discourage the trimming of whiskers as the dog is to have a natural look.

A number of years ago there was a campaign to eliminate foreign substances from the coat of dogs in the ring. Dogs were regularly excused when a foreign substance such as hair spray or chalk was found in the coat. While dogs are occasionally excused for foreign substances today, this does not happen with the same frequency as in the past. A number of judges will just place the offending dog at the end of the line either physically or in their own mind and not go through the stress of confrontation with an irate exhibitor.

GAIT

Each breed should have a gait that is peculiar to it and typical for the breed. Each dog must move like the other representatives of the breed if it is to be classified as a typical specimen of the breed. It would probably be too much of an overgeneralization to state that each breed is unique in its movement and that no other breed moves exactly as any other. Generally dogs that are built alike move alike. This can be seen in the Setters. With a common set of ancestors and common functional histories they tend to move in much the same manner. Some breeders will dispute this type of statement and point out that their breed is indeed a one-of-a-kind mover.

Some breeds do have unique movement or highly individual and identifiable gait. An outstanding example of this is seen in the Bulldog, whose easygoing, loose-jointed, shuffling roll is easily identified even by non-Bulldog breeders. Other distinctive gaits include the hackney action of the Miniature Pinscher and the high stepping movement of the Italian Greyhound and the Bedlington Terrier. The Afghan Hound has the free flowing, smooth gait that is the result of his great reach and strong powerful drive. The low Pembroke Welsh Corgi has strong reach and drive for such a short dog. The silhouette of the side gait of this dog is impressive for the strength of his movement.

While not every breed is as easily categorized as the several breeds mentioned above, the judge needs to be thoroughly familiar with the special gait of any individual breed as it is an integral part of what constitutes type in that breed.

TEMPERAMENT

The temperament is the personality of the dog. It is his psychological make-up and one of the elements that makes a dog unique and different from dogs of other breeds. Since it is an element of differentiation, it is an element of type.

Toy dogs in general are small, active, and animated. They endeavor to please their human companions as they should since this is the function for which they were bred. When a dog fails to accomplish this task, he shortly finds himself on the way to a new home.

Herding dogs were bred to herd animals and in so doing to carry out the commands of man. To achieve these goals the dog had to be subservient to the desires of man. He frequently was a one-man or one-family dog and a number of standards call attention to this quality of protectiveness. The standard for the Australian Cattle Dog states that "Whilst suspicious of strangers, must be amenable to handling in the show ring." The Lhasa Apso is characterized as being "chary of strangers." This aloofness is part of the personality of these breeds and dogs not demonstrating these personality traits would be atypical.

The standard for the Rottweiler states that he "should possess a fearless expression with a self assured aloofness that does not lend itself to immediate and indiscriminate friendships." It further states that "A judge shall dismiss from the ring any shy or vicious Rottweiler." When fearlessness passes over the line to aggressiveness, it is the responsibility of the judge to help the breeders correct this problem. This fearlessness is a part of the personality of the breed and dogs not demonstrating this quality are less than typical.

Shyness and viciousness are listed as faults in a number of breeds and these qualities are not considered typical for the breed. The Pembroke Welsh Corgi standard requires that the judge excuse from the ring any dog showing either of these two qualities. This is classified as unacceptable and atypical behavior for the breed and, therefore, eliminates a dog from further consideration.

SUMMARY

Type is then defined as a combination of those elements which distinguishes one breed of dog from another. It includes not only how the dog looks, but how it acts, and how it moves. All of these areas are important if the dog is to be a true and faithful representative of his breed.

The standing silhouette of the dog, whether in a show pose or free-standing, gives the initial impression to the judge and allows him to evaluate this aspect of type. The decision is that the dog looks like the breed, is a good representative of the breed, is recognizable as having some breed characteristics, or is so atypical that he is removed from serious consideration.

After the static evaluation of the dog is made, the judge must then evaluate the movement of the dog and determine if it is movement that is typical of that particular breed. It must be determined if the stride is the right length, if the balance between front and rear is correct for the breed, if the side movement is correct as well as the coming and going movement, and if a specimen with this balance of movement could accomplish the tasks for which the breed was originally created.

On the individual physical examination, the judge confirms his original opinion of the gait and its faults by examining the bone and muscle structure of the dog. If the original impression is not confirmed, the dog must be gaited again and reevaluated so that the question can be resolved. During this individual examination, the temperament of the dog can also be studied to determine the correctness for the breed.

After the various segments of the dogs have been studied independently, the judge must then reassemble the dog as a whole unit and not just a collection of parts. Some judges appear to have trouble judging the dog as a whole and dwell on the parts, giving undue weight to individual faults and failing to see and consider the dog as a whole living unit. Faults are certainly to be considered but they must be held in their proper place in the overall scheme of judging dogs.

Self-Test Questions

1. What is type?
2. What is the first step in evaluating a dog?
3. Are temperament and gait part of type?
4. Why is the skull-to-muzzle ratio important in analyzing head type?
5. What is the term used to describe the step-up between the muzzle and the skull?
6. What aspects are considered in evaluating ears?
7. What is the most important element of expression?
8. What aspects are considered in evaluating eyes?
9. Is it easier to detect bite problems when looking at the dog from the front or from the side?
10. What do many breeds consider to be the correct layback of the scapula?
11. What makes the Bulldog's front legs appear to be curved?
12. When no specific length is mentioned, what length is considered to be normal?
13. Which group of dogs has the greatest tuck-up?

Self-Test Questions

14. What is an open coat?
15. What is a broken coat?
16. Can all stripped coats be rolled?
17. What is temperament?
18. Do all exhibitors have a substantial working knowledge of the breed they are exhibiting?
19. Do all standards rate equally when it comes to being specific about the breed being described?
20. Why should a judge take into account the history of the breed when he is making his evaluations?
21. Why is type the single most important element in judging any breed?
22. Why is eye shape important?
23. Why is the size of the nose leather important when examining the head?
24. How do the length and shape of the neck affect the appearance of a dog?
25. What are some of the difficulties involved in evaluating a dog's neck?
26. What are some of the factors that can alter the angle at the point of shoulder?

The American Kennel Club

The creation of kennel clubs around the world was more the result of a growing need for regulation and record keeping than a desire on the part canine lovers to establish a new level of bureaucracy. The need existed and was felt and then the reality of these organizations came into being.

The earliest dog competitions were a far cry from what is conceived to be a dog show today. Early interest in dog competition was seen in the armies of fighting dogs used in the Mideastern wars in ancient times. These fighting dogs were trained and the competition was the war itself. The winner of this competition was the winning side in the war so the effectiveness of the training was extremely important. The outcome of modern-day field tests is of less consequence for those involved.

Another example of early dog sport was seen in lion and bear baiting. This lead to the creation and development of some breeds that had special talents for this type of work. The Bulldog is an example of this in that he was bred specifically to bait bears. His nose was foreshortened so that he would have a broad jaw which would aid greatly in holding on to his prey. The bulk of his weight was in his forequarters and the hindquarters were narrow. This enhanced his holding power, for when the bear shook, the lack of weight in the rear diminished the snapping effect which would tend to pull the dog loose. The foreshortening of the nose also prevented the nose from being

Canine education starts early at the Dog Museum. Roger Schlueter leads a discussion with visiting schoolchildren.

One source of canine research material is the library of the American Kennel Club.

embedded in the coat of the bear so that he could breathe more easily. The wrinkles of the forehead slowed any blood flow and kept the eyes clear.

Dog fighting itself was another form of competition and one that unfortunately has continued to the present day in a number of areas across the country. Dogs were especially bred for this type of competition much the same that fighting cocks were bred for fighting. The past breeding of fighting dogs has resulted in much of the breed-specific legislation that is causing the purebred dog world so many problems today.

In the mid 1800's rat-killing competitions were popular in England. Pit competitions were held in taverns in an effort to attract and hold patrons. Terriers were used for this type of fighting since they were ground dogs already used for the hunting of rodents. Individual dogs became quite famous as mass killers of rodents. The number of rats killed in a certain period of time brought honors to the dog and his master and profit to the tavern keeper.

Another early competition was among the field dogs, especially the Hounds. Their work in the field as Pointers, Retrievers, or Flushers brought attention and adulation. A scent Hound that could stay the trail was invaluable in a society in which a main source of meat was produced by hunting. These dogs were much more valuable to a family than a dog that killed rats in a tavern. However, egotism, pride, and the lure of wealth kept tavern competition keen.

Since fame depended on skills and skills depended on record keeping, a need was felt for something more than a personal set of records that might or might not reflect the true facts of the situation. Records of field achievements soon overshadowed other more frivolous competition and led to the first formal field trials.

The first officially recorded dog show competition took place in Newcastle-on-Tyne, England, on June 28 and 29, 1859. This show had a total entry of about 60. Entries included only Pointers and Setters which underscored the great interest in field-type dogs. These dogs were used for serious purposes rather than for frivolous ones. The rodent killers were left for tavern amusement only.

A second show was held the next year in 1860 in Birmingham. The total entry was 267 and divided the dogs into two Divisions. Division I was for Sporting dogs and Division II for all other dogs.

The Kennel Club of England was founded in 1873 and the first show held under its auspices took place between June 17 and June 20 in 1873. This show was held in the Crystal Palace in London. The Crystal Palace was the show place of the capital at that time so great attention was drawn to the show. Additional interest was stimulated as Queen Victoria was a great dog lover and kept many different breeds in the palace. Many of these breeds were exotic and were brought back from the newly conquered territories around the world. The entry at this show was 975. The following year in 1874 The Kennel Club established the first stud book and record keeping was a permanent part of the dog world.

THE UNITED STATES

The first stud book in the United States appeared in 1876. This was not the document of an official regulatory body, but rather the work of Arnold Burges. He published *The American Kennel and Sporting Field* which included a listing of 327 dogs. It was a modest beginning but did establish a pattern that has continued until the present day.

The first dog show in the United States was held on October 7, 1874 in Mineola, New York. This show was held under the rules of The Kennel Club of England. The second show was held the next day on October 8 in Memphis, Tennessee. This show was sponsored by the Tennessee Sportmen's Association and combined both bench and field competition under the rules of The Kennel Club of England. The Memphis Kennel Club held its centennial show on June 2, 1974 with a large panel of breeder judges and group prizes of $500 with the Best-in-Show prize of $2500.

The National American Kennel Club was founded in Chicago on January 26, 1876. Permanent headquarters were shortly after established in St. Louis. An official stud book was published which divided the dogs into two Divisions. Division I was for Sporting dogs and Division II was for Non-Sporting dogs. The orientation of this organization was more to field trials rather than to bench shows. Dr. Nicholas Rowe, who served as the first President, was also the driving force behind the record keeping and he maintained these books on an irregular basis until his death in 1896.

In 1884 the National American Kennel Club changed its name to the National Field Trial Club as it no longer had interest in bench shows. This move cleared the way for the establishment of the American Kennel Club.

On September 17, 1884 the representatives of twelve American and two Canadian kennel clubs met in Philadelphia to discuss the possibility of forming an organization that would be dedicated to bench show competition. At a follow-up meeting, reports were presented and the tentative name of the National Bench Show Association was changed to the American Kennel Club. Major J. M. Taylor of Lexington, Kentucky, was the first President. Elliot Smith of New York, New York, was First Vice-President, Samuel Coulson of Montreal, Canada, was Second Vice-President, Edward S. Porter of New Haven, Connecticut was Secretary, and G.N. Appold of Baltimore, Maryland, was Treasurer.

The second annual meeting was held May 19, 1885. A constitution committee was established and work was begun on breed standards and rules for holding dog shows. In 1887 the organization took over responsibility for the preparation of *The American Kennel Stud Book* that had previously been prepared by Dr. Rowe. The new name for the publication was *The American Kennel Club Stud Book*. In 1889 the representatives from the Canadian kennel clubs withdrew from the American Kennel Club and formed the Canadian Kennel Club.

In 1888 August Belmont, Jr. was elected the fourth President. His tenure altered the pattern of regularly changing the chief executive. He served for twenty-seven years, retiring in 1915. Alfred P. Vredenburg was elected Secretary in 1886 and served in this capacity or as Secretary-Treasurer until 1919. The long tenure of these two men moved the organization forward with great continuity and singleness of purpose.

In 1889 *The American Kennel Gazette* was established with James Watson as its first editor. He served until 1900. This publication was dedicated to matters pertaining to purebred dogs. *The American Kennel Gazette* continues today as one of the longest continuously published animal periodicals in the world.

An interesting historical note is that the American Kennel Club allowed individual membership in the club. This served as a continuing point of dissension and such membership was finally eliminated, but not until 1923.

The original championship point system was based on the total entry at a show rather than on the entry of an individual breed. This caused inequity since breeds with few entries could be finished more easily than breeds with larger entries. The present-day rules for championship were established in 1908. This included the winning of fifteen points under three different judges.

On May 26, 1908 the American Kennel Club was incorporated in the state of New York and the constitution and by-laws were adopted. The organization was now the legal and official representative of the dog world in the United States. The recognition of this now-official body facilitated the establishing of rules and regulations which were needed as show-giving clubs were proliferating across the country.

In 1909 the first Trial Boards were established. This was followed in 1923 by the publication of a set of rules to regulate dog shows and dog show judging. The first division of dogs into groups took place this same year. Five groups were established: Sporting, Working, Terrier, Toy, and Non-Sporting. Shortly thereafter the Sporting group was divided into the Sporting and Hound groups, making a total of six groups, an arrangement which continued for more than half a century. Group and Best-in-Show competition was also established. It should be noted that the first Best in Show was awarded in 1885 in Connecticut and was bestowed on a White Bull Terrier.

Rules and regulations followed rapidly and on a regular basis. After 1924 a veterinarian was required at every show. In 1925 judges were licensed to eliminate problems resulting from a lack of centralized control. The rule was relaxed in 1927 permitting anyone in good standing with the American Kennel Club to officiate as a judge pending approval of the club. The addition of the American Bred Class was also accomplished in 1927.

In 1929 *Pure Bred Dogs* was published as the first collection of breed standards. This publication continued until 1938 when the title was changed to *The Complete Dog Book*. In 1932 Children's Handling Classes were established and continued with this title until 1951 when the name was changed to Junior Showmanship. The year 1932 was when the official *Rules Applying to Registration and Dog Shows* first appeared. In 1934 the library was established at the headquarters of the American Kennel Club. In 1935 the one millionth dog was registered. It took fifty-one years to register one million dogs. At present more than one million dogs are registered each year.

Following World War II, interest in dog show competition became so keen that more than one hundred all-breed shows were held annually. In the 2000's there are now more than one thousand all-breed shows each year. This figure does not count specialty shows or field trials.

In 1946 Leonard Brumby, Sr. was appointed as the first field representative. At present there are about nineteen field representatives working in all parts of the country. In 1947 *Licensed Judges*, the first directory of judges, made its appearance. The title of this publication was later changed to *Dog Show Judges* while the current title is *Dog Show and Obedience Trial Judges*.

Between 1949 and 1970 the apprenticeship judge system was in operation. During this period of time, a person apprenticed in the ring under an already approved judge. Upon completing this program, the apprentice was approved to judge at regular shows. In 1951 a judge was expected to judge at a rate of twenty dogs an hour, but in 1960 this limit was raised to twenty-five dogs an hour with a total of 200 dogs per day. This number has subsequently been lowered to 175 dogs per day. In 1969 the Provisional Judging System was established and has continued with modifications up until present.

Progress and interest in purebred dogs continued over the decades and 1970 marked the first year in which one million dogs were registered in a single year. One million registrations annually has continued with few exceptions since that date.

Junior Showmanship was officially recognized by the American Kennel Club in 1971. In 1982 the Dog Museum of America was founded and was located at corporate headquarters in New York City. The museum moved to St. Louis, Missouri, in 1986 and later changed the name to The Dog Museum. With the move to St. Louis, attendance statistics greatly increased and the museum continues to expand both its collection and its physical facilities.

In 1983 the Working group was divided into the Working group and the Herding group. In 1984 the American

Kennel Club held its American Kennel Club Centennial Dog Show and Obedience Trial at the Civic Center in Philadelphia, Pennsylvania. The total entry was 8,075 dogs. The American Kennel Club and purebred dogs in the United States are officially into their second century.

JUDGING DOG SHOWS

*From **AKC Judging Application Process**, revised July 2000, courtesy of the American Kennel Club. (Be sure to check with AKC for the most current version).*

REQUIREMENTS

Individuals applying as new breed judges may apply for a maximum of up to 13 breeds on their first application and must meet the following criteria.

- In initial breeds must have 12 or more years of experience in the sport, bred and raised five or more litters in one breed; bred four or more champions in one breed. Litters and co-owned litters must have been whelped and raised on applicant's premises. The required four champions must be from litters whelped and raised on applicant's premises.
- If applicants do not meet the litter and/or champion criteria in the initial breed(s), they may apply under the "60 Point System," i.e., 15 years in the sport and achieve 60 points in each breed as outlined under the "60 Point System."

The following criteria is mandatory to apply for initial breed(s):

- Acted as assigned steward at least six times at AKC member and licensed shows.

- Completed six judging assignments at AKC-sanctioned matches, sweepstakes, and/or futuri ties (sweepstakes and futurities count as two matches).
- Viewed the AKC video on each breed required.
- Met AKC's occupational eligibility requirements.
- Successfully completed anatomy and procedural open-book tests.

THE 60 POINT SYSTEM

Only those breeds in which the applicant has documented experience in owning, breeding and exhibiting category will be granted on the first application; however, if applicant does not meet litter and/or champion requirements, a degree of flexibility may be employed by the reviewing staff to ensure that quality of experience, rather than quantity, is the determining factor in breeds granted. If the 60 Point System is used, applicants must have 15 years of documented experience in the sport and must achieve a total of 60 points per breed requested, using a combination of the following "enriching" factors:

Breeding, owning, and exhibiting elements (20 points for each). *Note: This assumes that using the 60 Point System the applicant does not meet both champion and litter requirements.*

- Bred at least four champions in breed(s) requested.
- Bred and raised five litters in breed(s) requested on his or her premises.
- Owned at least one dog in breed(s) requested that sired four champions. (Dog must have resided at applicant's home while used at stud.)
- Owned four dogs in breed(s) requested that earned championships while residing at applicant's home.
- Personally exhibited four dogs in breed(s) requested to their championships, earning all 15 points and both majors. This requirement is the same for owners and professional handlers.

- Personally exhibited two dogs in breed(s) requested as specials for a minimum of two years or approximately 60 showings. This requirement is the same for owners and professional handlers.
- Participated in Performance Events with two dogs of this breed for a minimum of two years.

Breed Specific Breeding, Owning and Exhibiting Elements (10 points for each).

- Competed in Junior Showmanship and can document having shown two or more dogs in breed(s) requested over a period of two or more years or approximately 60 showings.
- Owned two dogs of this breed(s) exhibited as specials, for a minimum of two years or approximately 60 showings.
- Member of household where five or more litters of this breed produced four or more champions but was not breeder of record.

Professional Experiences (Score 10 Points for each)

- Handled professionally or assisted professional handler for at least five years.
- Professionally groomed breeds in a show-related context: for a show kennel, for a professional handler, etc., for at least five years.
- Practiced canine health related profession for at least five years.
- Recognized author or frequent speaker on subjects related to purebred dogs.
- Instructor/teacher of purebred dog-related class-es for at least five years or approximately 60 classes.

Club Related or Educational Experience (Score 5 points for each)

- Active kennel club member. To qualify, applicant must have served as a club officer or on a show committee.

- Performed show-giving club services, such as committee work, site and ring preparation, and club educational programs.
- Attended institutes sponsored by knowledgeable organizations or parent clubs.
- Attended National Specialties and participated in judges' study groups.
- Presented parent club workshops, study groups or seminars on the breed(s) requested.
- Volunteered on behalf of regional or national breed club as mentor or presenter for parent club's educational programs or other credible educational programs.

INTERVIEW PROCESS

An application interview is mandatory. The Field Representative will screen the application to eliminate applying for breeds which the applicant seems unqualified to judge. Interviews must be scheduled through Judging Operations and copies of the required written tests must be on file in the office. During the interview applicants will be reminded that the interview does not guarantee automatic acceptance of the breed discussed.

The application interview will include, but not be limited to the following:

- If dates provided for litters/champions/stewarding/matches are from more than 10 years ago, there must be a discussion of current activities.
- Applicant must clarify any discrepancies in answer.
- Applicant must provide answers to all questions; those left blank require an explanation.
- Discuss strengths, weaknesses and differences with-in breed(s).
- Discuss and demonstrate proper use of wicket/

scale/dentition (if applicable).

- Discuss mandatory test results.
- Review procedural observation and breed evaluation forms.
- Review rules, regulations and guidelines.
- Discuss proper procedure for handling protests, disqualifications and excuses.
- Discuss importance of positive reports from Field Representatives and mentors in being granted regular status.

All applicants accepted for full or partial approval will be published in the *Gazette* the month following the Board meeting. Provisional status will be granted 30 days following publication of the Board's acceptance of an application provided that the applicant receives a passing grade on the breed standard test(s). If an applicant fails any test, all breeds will be placed on hold for three months, and the missed questions must be reviewed with a Field Representative before continuing to process the application.

Regular Status Requirements:

- Complete five assignments in each provisional breed, demonstrating sufficient competence in the breeds most recently granted.
- Unlimited assignments may be accepted.
- Additional provisional assignments may be required to achieve regular status.
- Must have been observed three times by different Field Representatives. (Judging Operations staff may reduce this requirement in breeds with consistently small entries.)

ADDITIONAL BREEDS

Requirements:

On the second application individuals may apply for only the number of breeds granted on the initial application (one-for-one policy). On the third application individuals may request up to a maximum of 13 breeds. The following criteria is mandatory to apply for additional breed(s):

- Have been granted regular status in all provisional breeds.
- At least one year must have elapsed since last Board action.
- If disapproved, one year must have elapsed from the Board date and must have completed three conformation judging assignments before submitting another application.
- Have reviewed AKC video on each breed requested.

Enriching Components.
Some combination of at least four of the "enriching" components, when well documented, must be included:

- Experience owning, breeding, and exhibiting all requested breeds.
- Attending Regional Specialties.
- Attending National Specialties and participating in judges' study groups (count as two).
- Attending Seminars.
- Attending institutes sponsored by knowledgeable organizations or parent clubs.
- Judging AKC sanctioned matches, sweepstakes, and/or futurities in each breed requested.
- Selecting and working with qualified mentors. Mentor reports must be on file with the Judging Operations Department early in the process. Mentoring will consist of the following opportunities:
  - Tutoring and guiding the applicant in breed knowledge.
  - Continuing the learning exchange throughout the applicant's provisional status.

- In-ring observations meeting the following criteria:
  a) may observe only under judges who have been

approved for the specific breed(s) for a minimum of five years, or approved breeder judges of 10 or more years' experience in the breed(s).

b) If the judge under whom you are observing does not meet these criteria, this observation cannot be submitted in connection with your additional breed application:
   - must have adequate entries for the specific breed(s).
   - must have permission of the Show Chairman and the adjudicating judge.
   - must wear an Observer's Badge while inthe ring.
   - must limit observations to two hours under any one judge.
   - must properly complete an observa tion form (indicating show date, name and show number, location, breed(s) observed, entry in each breed) and present it to the adjudicating judge for signature and any voluntary com ments. All observation forms should accompany the additional breed application.

Interview Process:
An application interview is mandatory. Prior to the interview, paperwork should be sent to the office for verification that requirements have been met. A copy of the application will then be sent to the Field Staff member conducting the interview. The Field Representative will screen the application to eliminate applying for breeds which the applicant seems unqualified to judge. Interviews must be scheduled through Judging Operations. Only those Field Staff who have personal knowledge of the applicants' qualification will be voting on their application.

The application will include, but not be limited to, the following:

- Breed-specific seminar as well as seminars listed multiple times.
- Mentor participation will be verified.
- Applicant must provide answers to all questions; those left blank require an explanation.
- Discuss strengths, weaknesses and differences within the breed(s).
- Discuss and demonstrate proper use of wicket/ scale/dentition if applicable.
- Review rules, regulations, policies and guidelines if applicable.
- Discuss proper procedure for handling protests, disqualifications and excuses.
- Discuss importance of positive reports from Field Representatives and mentors in being granted regular status.

All applicants for full or partial approval will be published in the *Gazette* the month following the Board meeting. Provisional status will be granted 30 days following publication of the Board's acceptance of an application provided that the applicant receives a passing grade on the breed standard test(s). If an applicant fails any test, all breeds will be placed on hold for three months, and the missed question(s) must be reviewed with a Field Representative before continuing to process the application.

Regular Status Requirement:

- Complete five assignments in each provisional breed.
- Unlimited assignments may be accepted.
- Additional provisional assignments may be required to achieve regular status.
- Must have been observed three times by different Field Representatives. The Judging Operations Department may reduce this requirement in breeds with consistently small entries.

RE-EVALUATION

New Breed and Approved Breed applicants, who wish to contest the Board's decision of partial approval or denial, may request a re-evaluation by writing to the Judging Operations Department. Requests for re-evaluation must be filed within 60 days of receiving notification of the Board's decision and should include significant additional information not submitted in the original application. All additional information must refer to experience that preceded the submission of the application. Re-evaluation entails a review of the entire application.

Re-evaluation is acted upon by a Staff Committee, and if change is deemed appropriate, a recommendation will then be submitted to the Board for approval. Applicants who wish to contest the re-evaluation decision may request a review by the Judges' Review Committee.

ALTERNATIVE METHOD FOR JUDGES WITH THREE OR MORE GROUPS

The alternative method allows applicants to submit a written synopsis rather than completing the additional breed forms. This method is for qualified judges with three or more complete groups who wish to apply for one-half to an entire Group. To qualify for the alternative process, judges must meet the following criteria:

- Have regular status in three or more Groups.
- Have judged their most recently approved breeds at least 10 times following granting of regular status.
- Must have positive reports on file from a minimum of 10 Field Representatives.

Applicants must submit a brief synopsis outlining their background and educational preparation to judge the breeds requested and why they should be approved to judge the breeds. If the applicant is determined to be qualified for the advancement, Judging Operations will set up an interview to be conducted by two Field Representatives, or one Field Representative and one member of the Judging Operations staff. The interview will cover basic breed knowledge and essential breed characteristics. Each interviewer will submit a recommendation for final determination, after which breed standard tests will be administered. Provisional status will be granted upon successful completion of the appropriate tests.

Group judges who do not meet the criteria for the alternative process may apply under the regular system for up to 13 breeds. There will be no re-evaluation or review process available under the alternative system.

PERFORMANCE EVALUATION TESTING

In the fall of 1987 the American Kennel Club instituted a program of hands-on testing in order to evaluate ring procedures and practical application ability of judges applying for additional breeds. The pilot program lasted about one year before a more permanent, but still experimental, program was established.

The hands-on panel consisted of two approved judges and the AKC Field Representative. From a field of twelve dogs, this group selected a test class of eight dogs. This class ideally contained two dogs of quality, four average quality dogs, and two poor-quality specimens. The candidate was expected to place the dogs in approximately the same order as the committee did and to explain his placements. This program continued until 1994.

BREED EVALUATIONS JUDGING PROGRAM

In 1995 the Board of Directors approved an experimental judging approval system for advancement beyond the first group. The program was called "Breed Evaluations" and was entirely optional in that only judges volunteering for the program would be involved. The new program did not change the current system in any way. This gave group judges wishing to advance an option.

The following special features characterize the system:

1. The foundation of the system is based on breed discussions, on evaluations of representative breed specimens, and on judging competency based on class judging.
2. The intent is to provide a system based on mutual understanding and the absence of surprises. This is accomplished by understanding in part an applicant's knowledge of breeds before accepting (1) an application for specific breeds and (2) a plan for group advancement.
3. Pre-application breed competency is established during (1) multiple interviews with Staff involving breed discussions and the critique of one or two breed specimens of one or more breeds and (2) evaluation of at least one class of representative specimens of one or more breeds.
4. Post-application competency permits the applicant to advance from provisional approval to regular approval based in part on breed discussions with Staff immediately following provisional breed assignments

The Breed Evaluation (BE) Option was added to the current approval system for judges approved for at least one group. The focus was performance-based with Class Breed Evaluations (CBEs) and Individual Breed Evaluations (IBEs) and interviews at the core of the system. Approval was agreed to in advance assuming satisfactory performance and was based on one, two, three, or four applications for the group. Applicants prepared to demonstrate judging competency by performance could thus be advanced at a defined rate. This program was deleted in 1997.

The Senior Conformation Judges Association and the American Kennel Club have both initiated annual week-long seminars designed basically for new judges and judges applying for additional breeds. As these program develop, the organizers will make modifications and may well introduce additional new areas of study. In addition, the American Kennel Club is preparing to introduce a Mentor Program that will use the most senior judges to help new judges work into the system.

The Dog Museum in St. Louis, Missouri, offers an excellent opportunity to study the visual history of dogs. This is a photograph of the Westminster Kennel Club Gallery in Jarville House.

Self-Test Questions

1. What was the first unofficial dog competition?
2. For what purpose was the Bulldog bred?
3. What animals did dogs kill in tavern competition?
4. When was the first dog show held in England?
5. When was The Kennel Club of England founded?
6. Who was England's greatest publicist for purebred dogs in the nineteenth century?
7. When was the first dog show held in the United States?
8. Where was the first centennial dog show held?
9. Where was the National American Kennel Club founded?
10. In what year was the organizational meeting of the future American Kennel Club held?
11. What is the name of the official monthly publication of the American Kennel Club?
12. What breed won the first Best in Show?
13. What is the title of the book containing the histories and the standards for each breed?

Self-Test Questions

14. What was the title of the judge-training program used in the 1950's and the 1960's?

15. When did the first stud book appear in the United States?

16. Who served as the first president of the National American Kennel Club?

17. What were the two divisions of the stud book for the National American Kennel Club?

18. Who was the first president of the American Kennel Club?

19. When were the present-day rules for championship established?

20. When were the first Trial Boards established?

21. How many field representatives work throughout the United States?

22. What was the apprenticeship judge system?

23. When was Junior Showmanship officially recognized by the American Kennel Club?

Judging

To hold a dog show, a certain number of elements must be present. This would, of course, include the single most important element which would be the dog. Next would be the handler who is responsible for showing and controlling the exhibit, and last is the judge who is supposed to be an expert in the breed and the individual who is capable of giving an unbiased evaluation of the exhibit. This unbiased evaluation is based on years of study and experience in the breed and an ability to apply this knowledge in a practical way to the judging of individual dogs. Still another important individual at the show and the one who makes things run smoothly is the superintendent or the show secretary. These last individuals are charged with the responsibility of doing the general preparation, the book work, and the heads and tails of the detail work.

PURPOSE

Judging is just another aspect of breeding quality dogs, although most exhibitors do not look upon judging as an integral part of their breeding program. They would, however, be well advised to so consider this aspect of the overall program as an important segment of breeding.

There are really few longtime breeder-exhibitors who do not consider the evaluation of their breeding stock by impartial, knowledgeable individuals as a significant phase in the improvement of their stock. It can be assumed that a dedicated breeder does not go to the expense and strain of participating in the show circuits for the ribbons and prizes that are won. If this were the case, that individual would be well advised to buy such items through a trophy company and save thousands of dollars each year.

Since prizes and ribbons have little value in themselves one must consider the value of championship points. These by themselves are really no more significant than the ribbons. They are, however, of collective importance in that they reflect an historical evaluation of an individual dog by a number of impartial evaluators. When individuals with somewhat different backgrounds and training all select the same dog as being outstanding, it is a testimony to the breeding skills of the exhibitor and is thus evidence that his theories and talents as a breeder are recognized by others.

The purpose then of judging is to participate in the betterment of the breeding of purebred dogs. This demands that those who undertake the charge of judging do so with the most serious intent of purpose, for what they do in the ring can have important and long-lasting consequences on the quality of dogs in the future. If an individual does not have these goals in mind, he is ill advised to undertake a career as a judge at dog shows.

Integrity is as important in judging as is knowledge and experience. If the judge does not deliver an impartial, knowledgeable evaluation of a dog, he is not serving the dog world and should certainly not be in a position where his actions can have influence. Not only must the judge have impartiality and integrity, but he must never say or do anything that would raise a question about either of these two qualities. It is impossible to be somewhat impartial and to have basically essential integrity. It is all or nothing. Giving the impression of being partial to a certain dog or exhibitor is professionally as wrong as being partial. Judges who lack these essential qualities of professionalism should not be in the ring.

THE JUDGE

Who should judge and why any particular individual should judge are always interesting questions and ones that are frequently asked of both new and experienced judges. The answers run from the idealistic to the egotistical and are indicative of the reasons why there is the variety in judging that has always been present.

One answer that is frequently given is that "I wanted to improve my breed." This individual certainly feels that he has a great deal to contribute to a breeding program. This may or may not be the truth of the matter, but if the individual sincerely feels that this is true it is a valid reason. Another statement that is occasionally heard is "I wanted to be able to go over a lot of different dogs in my breed to see why these dogs do so much more winning than mine." This statement would appear to be a truthful one, but hardly indicates a sound reason for becoming a judge. These statements would explain why an individual might apply for his original breed, but would give no evidence why this individual would seek to add additional breeds to his judging schedule.

Another explanation heard is that "I had been handling dogs for so long that I was tired of running around the ring and wanted to stay in the dog game but needed to do something less tiring." This is judging by default and not a really valid reason for being a judge. Judging will also be somewhat of a surprise for this individual since judging is physically tiring. Judging dogs at the rate of twenty-six to twenty-eight dogs per hour, as they are frequently being scheduled today, plus a group or two allows little time to sit down and rest. The exhibitor usually has time to sit down and relax sometime during the day.

Another statement that is heard is that "I have done it all in my breed and there is just nowhere else to go. I have bred for many years, have produced dozens of champions including Group and Best-in-Show winners and there is nothing left to accomplish. Maybe now I can help someone else get started." This is certainly a noble way of thinking and this individual may indeed make a significant contribution to a given breed.

When an individual decides to become a judge he will also have to determine if he is doing this for commercial purposes. If his general income has come from dog-related activities, he will need an income from judging or from some other source. While it takes years of judging experience and the ability to judge multiple groups to earn a living as a judge, an individual can supplement an income from other sources with the fees he earns from his judging.

Some individuals charge no fee over their expenses. These individuals do so because they either have an income independent of revenues that might be produced from judging or they are involved in some other phase of the dog world that would preclude their charging a fee. One such case would be that of a judge who would also be a club delegate to the American Kennel Club which disallows delegate membership for anyone who is commercially involved with dogs. While this rule has been discussed many times over the years, it has not been modified at the time of the publication of this book.

Many judges who are able to judge fewer than all the dogs in one group charge a certain amount for each dog judged which will help defray their travel and living expenses for the assignment. Some other judges charge neither fees nor expenses, but there are not many of these individuals. Other judges charge expenses plus a contribution to their favorite charity. Still others turn back to the club a portion of their check to be used for trophies at a future show. There are many different ways in which judging expenses are handled and probably additional ones will be added in the future.

The term *professional judge* is used in different ways by different groups of individuals. Since the term seems to give higher standing to the group that uses it, it should have some sort of definition. Many judges who judge for a fee say that the term defines that they are career judges and make significant contributions to the field. There are other judges who have similar experience and training who feel that they are every bit as professional as the for-fee judges. This group resents being classified as amateur judges based merely on the fact that they do not charge a fee.

It might be well advised to use the term *professional* for any judge, regardless of whether or not he charges a fee, who has judged for a number of years and judges on an ongoing and regular basis. The judge who has only an assignment or two per year in his local area would not fall in this category.

THE PSYCHOLOGY OF JUDGING

Not everyone is suited to the conditions that are involved in a career as a judge. Many individuals are quite surprised by the strain of travel. Going to a dog show as an exhibitor presents one kind of strain, but after years involved in showing the exhibitor is so well adjusted to these activities that he does not even realize that they bring much added stress into his life.

Going to the shows as a judge presents a different set of conditions. First, you are going without the company of your dogs. This has both good and weak points. The dogs have always been good company and have given pleasure, but it is nice not to have to groom several dogs, feed or force feed, and exercise dogs in the rain. The travel strain of judging is on a different level since this involves a great deal of air travel. Air travel gets more expensive each year and the congestion in airports and with airline schedules becomes ever more complicated. Delays in one airport, even if it is not included on the judge's itinerary, can result in delays at another airport which can even lead to a missed connection. Switching air carriers at a major hub airport can be exasperating if a flight arrives late and passenger traffic is heavy on the concourses. Switching from a large jet to a small commuter plane usually requires switching terminals.

Getting from the airport to the motel used to mean trying to identify the club member assigned to the chore of picking up the judges. More often than not at present clubs do not furnish this service and the judge must catch a courtesy van, an airport shuttle, or a taxi. The longer a judge travels, the more familiar he becomes with each air terminal and he is able to find all these services easily since he has used them so often at all major airports.

Motel accommodations range from the elegant to the adequate and at times to the less than adequate. Rich clubs are usually not the ones that provide the best accommodations and this is one of the reasons they are rich. Best accommodations are usually provided by those clubs in which another judge is in charge of hospitality. They fully understand the rigors of travel and the real need for a good night's sleep, especially between a two-day assignment. When the room is minimal, it is sometimes the result of the fact that there simply are no better accommodations in the area where the show is being held.

Judges' hospitality dinners also can cause needless strain whether they are held the night before the show or following Best in Show. The biggest complaint about these dinners is that they are held too late. For someone who may have traveled across one or two time zones, an 8:00 PM dinner is just too late. One judge refuses to accept dinner invitations if the dinner is scheduled after 7:00 PM and is not held in the hotel where the judges are staying. Logistics of getting the judges from the motel to the dinner site prove to be beyond the organizational talents of many clubs. The organizer often fails to have adequate transportation available and cannot remember who has made reservations and who has not. The same situation is frequently the case on the morning of the show in trying to get the judges to the show grounds. On many occasions one judge will take command and get the convoy organized rather than stand there and just be frustrated.

Show sites range from excellent to unsatisfactory. Outside shows can be true disasters. In the summer they can be too hot and provide no shade. Late fall and early spring shows in the upper Midwest can run from pleasant conditions to tornado-like weather or provide real blizzards. At least the exhibitors can warm up in a car or a motor home, but the judge cannot leave the ring to do this. New judges are frequently surprised by these conditions and their inability to do anything to change them.

The last logistical challenge of the day is getting back from the show site to the motel or to the airport. Many show chairmen simply forget that this has to be done. At the last minute they are running around trying to find some exhibitor who is going by the airport and is willing to drop off a judge. More than one judge has missed the last flight out because such an exhibitor was unfamiliar with the airport and did not know how to get there without getting lost. The added expense of an extra night is on the judge since he did not include this charge in his expenses.

In spite of these difficulties, the vast majority of clubs provide faithful and good service in dealing with the judges. It is only occasionally that difficulties arise, but when they do, it does cause stress on what should otherwise be an enjoyable assignment.

RING STRESSES

If the judge arrives at the ring agitated and unhappy about things that have already happened, it is going to be a bad day and a long one. When this is the case, he must correct his attitude if he is to do a fair and impartial job of judging.

Big outdoor rings provide an excellent opportunity to judge the movement of large dogs.

Decision making is a taxing process for everyone. For some it seems natural and easy while others dwell on each individual decision and agonize over each element and still cannot feel comfortable about their final choices. Many of these individuals who suffer in the decision-making process know which is the better of the two dogs and which one should go up, but they find it extremely difficult to say a simple "One" and "Two." A few years ago, a longtime breeder-exhibitor started judging. He knew the three breeds he was to judge very well and knew which dogs should go up on any particular day. His decisions were agonizing for both him, the exhibitors, and the ringside spectators as well. He would judge each class two or three times, but it was still not easy. After a few years, when he stopped judging, a good friend told him that was the best thing he could have done for the dog world. His indecisiveness resulted not from a lack of breed knowledge, but from his not wanting to offend friends, put too much emphasis on his own breeding line, or reward longtime competitors. All of these were invalid reasons and his decision to retire from judging was a wise one.

The ability to make quick decisions is a prime requisite of a judge. He has a very small amount of time to make each individual decision. It would be wise to limit new judges to no more than twenty-two dogs an hour for the first six to ten assignments since this is about the speed at which new judges seem to work best. One of the reasons that new judges do not move along as rapidly as a more experienced judge is that they have not seen all the faults or combination of faults in their brief judging career. Longtime judges of a breed have already seen almost every possible combination of faults and have their own priority list well established and can make their placements quite efficiently. Occasionally an experienced judge will comment to a colleague that "I saw something new today." This will almost be said in surprise for he thought he had already seen every combination of good qualities and faults in that breed.

Judging at a rate of twenty-five dogs an hour sounds like it would provide almost two and one-half minutes per dog. This is not the case since various classes must be brought in and armbands must be checked. The judge's book must be marked, and time must be provided for photographs. This brings the real time allocated for each dog to about one minute and a half. During this time, the judge must analyze the type, balance, and soundness of the dog as well as find and prioritize the faults to be weighed against the good qualities of the dog, and he must also determine if the dog limps or has any disqualifying faults. Years of experience make this possible and easy, but to the novice judge it does present a challenge. Any judge may request from the superintendent that he be scheduled for fewer than twenty-five dogs per hour. This must be done in writing several weeks before the show. Evaluation reports will make note if a judge is consistently late in his judging.

If a Provisional Judge's first assignment is in his own local area he will find that the ring will be full of longtime friends and competitors, all of whom will expect to win because they either have the best dog or because of the long relationship with the judge. The novice judge must realize that there will only be one truly happy exhibitor that day and that will be the owner of the dog that goes Best of Breed. Degrees of happiness will go down from there. The judge will more frequently be asked reasons for his placements on his first assignments than he will be at later shows. When many exhibitors ask for an explanation, they really do not want to hear the judge's answer but rather give themselves an opportunity to tell the judge what an excellent dog they have. A knowledgeable exhibitor should be able to look at the dogs placed ahead of him in line and those placed behind him and know where the judge put his emphasis for that evaluation. If the quality of the dogs was poor or very uneven, this could make an understanding more difficult, but again a knowing exhibitor should realize this as well as the judge. It is usually the novice exhibitors who regularly ask for explanations. Longtime breeders use their eyes and know the reason. However, if the judging is poor, no one may fully understand the placements, including the judge himself.

Once the decision is made about which dogs go first, second, third, and fourth, the judge must move promptly and efficiently to finish the details of this class and move on to the next class. When the judge is indecisive and anguishes over the decision before it is made and continues to rehash it during the next class, he will effectively lose control of the ring as he will be looking at the wrong dogs in the next class. This will only add to the confusion and confound the exhibitors. Those individuals who have difficulty making decisions promptly and moving on rapidly to the next challenge will find judging a very stressful and unrewarding profession. Breed knowledge is of extreme importance, but so also is decisiveness. The indecisive judge, merely by being indecisive, opens himself to challenges from the exhibitor. These challenges can be either real or more subtle through the use of body language. Many wily handlers maintain that they can easily control this type of judge and will frequently enter under such judges not because they respect their opinion, but rather because they can be controlled and will award wins rather than run the risk of a confrontation.

Experienced judges have already adapted to the strains and stresses of judging and work comfortably in this atmosphere. Novice judges must anticipate the problems involved in judging as best they can and come up with personal solutions in advance if they possibly can. The first year or two of judging will produce more pressure than in later years when the judge will be able to say, "I have not seen anything new for a long time."

PREPARING TO JUDGE

Preparations to judge under the present rules and regulations start at least ten years before the novice judge enters the ring for his first assignment. Of greatest importance in this preparation is the first-hand knowledge that an individual gets from being a breeder and exhibitor. There is very little else that can provide such valuable knowledge.

The standard of the breed is the basic building block for the judge. He must know the standard thoroughly and fully comprehend what it says as well as what it means. Unusual vocabulary must be mastered as well as the intricacies of faults and disqualifications. The formal testing procedure should help in this area, but many well experienced judges go over their standards each time they judge no matter how many years' experience they have in the breed. This is to be expected and is only fair to the exhibitor who is paying for the judge's opinion.

In addition to the standard, the judge must be thoroughly familiar with the history and development of the breed. This information will have been covered in the oral interview, but should be reviewed regularly. The historical development explains why the dog is what he is today and helps clarify the standard when it is ambiguous. Many standards are little help in sorting out dogs as some of the standards are so poorly written. They are not clear and sometimes do not even say what they intend to say. Some are vague while others are too precise, making it sound as if there is really no leeway in one area or another. Some standards have long lists of faults and categorize them as faults, serious faults, and very serious faults and call for appropriate penalties. If one interprets these standards literally, he would have to fault-judge that breed and discount the good qualities of the individual dog. Fault judging is negative in its approach, but that is what these few standards are really telling the judge to do.

Most breeds have at least one book dealing with the history and development of the breed. A few of the more popular breeds have several such books. These books vary in quality and in the information they contain about the breed. The reader must weigh the information contained in one book against that contained in other reference books and against the general knowledge of longtime breeders. There are also a number of good general reference books on the market as well as the publications of the American Kennel Club. A serious and dedicated judge will build a library of his own so he will have ready access to this type of historical information.

One of the most significant elements of canine education in recent years is the video-slide shows prepared by parent clubs under the auspices of the American Kennel Club. This has been an outstanding contribution to the study of different breeds. These video programs, while somewhat uneven in quality and presentation, are excellent and worthwhile. Owning each tape would be ideal, but costs make this impossible for most judges. Many all-breed clubs have a standing subscription for this series and use them for educational programs at club meetings and allow members to check out these videos in library fashion. This is a valuable service provided by these clubs.

General seminars were popular in the seventies and in the early eighties, but have more recently given way to breed-specific seminars presented by specialty clubs. These usually provide satisfactory opportunities to hear breeders discuss the breed as well as provide an opportunity to go over a number of examples of the breed that are of show quality. These breeder panels have been known to disintegrate into arguments between competing exhibitors.

One aspect of informal education that has all but disappeared is grooming-area training. When exhibitors used to set up all their crates and grooming equipment in one area, it was easy to circulate during the day and talk with breeders and handlers and learn in a relaxed atmosphere many details about the breed. Whether the information was good and correct had to be determined by the person seeking the information, but it was one source that was readily available. This situation almost does not exist today. The advent of the van and the motor home eliminated the need to move a string of dogs into a centralized area. At most shows today, the only exhibitors in the grooming areas are the novices who have not as yet made the financial commitment to motor homes. While these novices are usually very enthusiastic and willing to talk about their breed, their knowledge is so limited that it cannot be relied upon. Many times it is really misinformation.

One of the requirements on a judge's application is to discuss the breed with knowledgeable individuals, either breeders or judges of the breed. If one is sincere about learning, this is an opportunity to learn a great deal about the breed, especially about the problems that exist in the breed at the moment. Breeders frequently will not mention these problems, especially if they have them in their line, but an impartial judge will discuss them. The applicant needs to schedule an appointment with one of these experts and not try to catch him between classes at a show. Going to such an interview cold is unprofessional and a discourtesy to the individual who is willing to help with the furtherance of another's career. Preparation for such a session should include a review of the history and function of the breed and of the breed standard. A copy of the standard should be taken to the meeting. A lot can be learned from these interviews that may relieve more than one tense moment at the time of decision making in the ring.

With the exception of individuals who have made their living as professional handlers, everyone starts out as a breeder judge. He starts in a breed in which he has the maximum amount of experience and training. He has been a breeder of the breed and a longtime exhibitor. He will have stewarded in the breed ring and will have had some experience at judging at matches or sweepstakes. Breeder judges are thoroughly trained even if it is only informally.

Many exhibitors love to show under breeder judges as they feel they are the more knowledgeable. Other exhibitors will shy away from such judges as they feel that the breeder judge gets hung up on a particular aspect of the dog and fails to see the dog as a whole unit. Breeder judges occasionally do become obsessed with a certain aspect of the dog. Sometimes it is a quality in which their own particular line excelled. At other times it is a quality with which they had continued difficulty and never did get a handle on the problem. While it is thorough judging to note special areas of concern, it is bad judging to give undue emphasis to these specific points to the exclusion of other points of greater significance. Every part of the dog is important, but it would be unusual for any part to overshadow all other parts and invalidate the dog as a whole.

When those who start out as breeder judges move to other breeds in which they do not have years of firsthand experience, they become generalists or general type judges. Their knowledge in these breeds is mostly secondhand experience. They are forced to rely almost exclusively on the knowledge of others and must learn how to evaluate the information they obtain from others. With firsthand experience it is easy to sort out information, but when it is secondhand experience it is more difficult. This is precisely where some judges get into trouble and give the appearance that they are not consistent in their judging. This is usually the result of a failure to get the proper perspective on the breed in general. If the judge is conscientious he should be able to master this situation. If not he will continue to have difficulty in progressing with his judging in new areas.

The true generalist is the all-rounder who has reached the career level of being able to judge all breeds. Judges who are qualified to do this type of judging usually number about twenty. Some years it may be as high as twenty-five and at other times as low as a dozen. It takes years of experience to attain this level of sophistication so the all-rounders are usually among the most senior judges in the country. Most of them are willing to share their knowledge and help younger and newer judges when they are asked to do so. They are very good at answering specific questions since they have this detailed knowledge.

Whatever one's aspirations may be in judging, the preparation is the same. The individual must have gained firsthand experience in his breed, he must have mastered the books and articles relating to the history and function of the specific breed, and he must be thoroughly familiar with the standard. He must also be completely familiar with ring procedures and the mechanics of judging so that these elements will not distract from the real job of the judge, which is evaluating and placing the dogs. If he is unwilling or incapable of doing all these things, then a career in judging should not be undertaken.

During the day of the show the judge works closely with the volunteer members of the show committee. The committee can only relax after the show is over.

Self-Test Questions

1. Is judging a part of breeding programs?
2. How important is impartiality in judging?
3. What is a valid reason for becoming a judge?
4. What travel problems must be anticipated by the judge?
5. At what rate can most new judges judge?
6. When will the judge most frequently be asked about his placements?
7. What is one cause of unhappiness about placements?
8. How important is the body language of an exhibitor?
9. What type of seminars are popular today?
10. What effect has the motorhome had on the dog show world?
11. Of what value are championship points?
12. What is the purpose of judging?

Self-Test Questions

13. What are three important qualities of a judge?
14. What is the definition of a professional judge?
15. What conditions should you consider before you decide to become a judge?
16. What kinds of stresses can you expect when you are a judge?
17. What is one primary requisite of being a judge?
18. What situations can cause a judge to lose control of the ring?
19. What is one of the requirements on a judge's application?
20. At what level of judging (other than individuals who have made their living as professional handlers) does a judge begin?
21. What four areas of preparation must a person go through before becoming a competent judge?

In the Ring

Establishing and running an efficient ring is an absolute necessity. It is a basic element of professionalism and a courtesy to the exhibitors. The judge has ultimate responsibility for the original setup of the ring and for the smooth-running function of all activities that take place therein during the hours of judging. Anything that goes wrong in the ring during judging is attributed to the judge whether or not he actually made the mistake. An original mistake made by the superintendent or the show secretary in setting up the ring is a mistake of the judge since he did not correct it before he started his assignment. If a steward allows the wrong dog in a class it is the the fault of the judge for not having caught the error. If the steward lays out the wrong ribbons and the judge hands them out it is his responsibility. The judge is all powerful when it comes to ring mechanics and entirely responsible for any error.

RING MECHANICS

The American Kennel Club has established minimum measurements for the size of rings. Small dogs are to be shown in rings no smaller than 20 by 30 feet while larger dogs have a minimum ring size of 30 by 40 feet. These rings may be larger and really need to be if classes are large or there will not be sufficient room to gait all dogs as the first dog in line will have run up on the last dog in line before he even has had a chance to get started. In cases where there is an extremely large class, the judge has the

(Above): An efficient ring arrangement, as the placement markers are to the right of the judge's table.The next class can be assembled while placements are recorded. (Below): An inefficient ring layout, as placement markers are to the left of the judge's table. This arrangement prevents the next class from entering the ring until the previous class has left.

option of dividing the class. The class is usually first assembled and then divided by armband numbers. A class may be divided by halves or thirds. Some dogs will need to step out of the ring to be called back so that the first section may be judged. The judge should hold for recall a number of dogs from each division. He should hold five from the first cut in case the remaining divisions are not of the same quality and to allow leeway in case one of the dogs starts limping. It is probably wise to hold about four dogs from each of the other divisions so that all exhibitors feel that they have received the same evaluation and treatment. This will also insure that the four best dogs will be awarded the placements.

Once it had been determined that the ring size is correct, the judge should check the entrance gate to make sure it is located in the most efficient place so that it will not allow dogs from two rings to congregate in the same area. It is best if the gate is located next to the outside ring steward's table and close to the judge's so if questions arise the judge does not have to walk the length of the ring to get the necessary information from the stewards.

The judge's table should be so located that the placement numbers are to the right of the table. This arrangement places the entrance to the left and allows the next class to assemble while ribbons are awarded. The greatest problem in ring efficiency at dog shows is, was, and will always be that of getting the exhibitor to show his armband to the judge. Reading an armband number running around the back of an exhibitor's arm who is standing at an angle talking to another exhibitor allows for errors. Old professionals do this as frequently as do the novice exhibitors. Repeated requests to superintendents asking them to change the ring the morning of the show easily establishes the pattern that you want for your own ring.

Before starting judging on the day of the show, the

judge should walk the ring to make sure that there is nothing in the ring that will hurt the dog or distract him while he is gaiting. This is especially important at cluster shows when the rings might not have been cleaned thoroughly since the previous show. If the show is an outside one, the judge should make note of any holes or hollows that might trip up an exhibitor. He should avoid using this part of the ring, but should also call each exhibitor's attention to the problem.

Indoor shows normally make use of mats to give both the dog and the exhibitor sufficient traction. It is the judge's responsibility to make sure that the mats are flat to the floor with no buckles or gaps and that corners and overlapping sections are carefully taped. The mats are laid out in a rectangle with one mat running diagonally across

This is an efficient layout for the ring.
Placement markers are to the right when facing the judge's table.
1. Ring gate. 2. Judge's table. 3. Examining table. 4. Placement markers.
5, 6, 7. Gaiting triangle. 9. Side for dogs waiting to be examined.

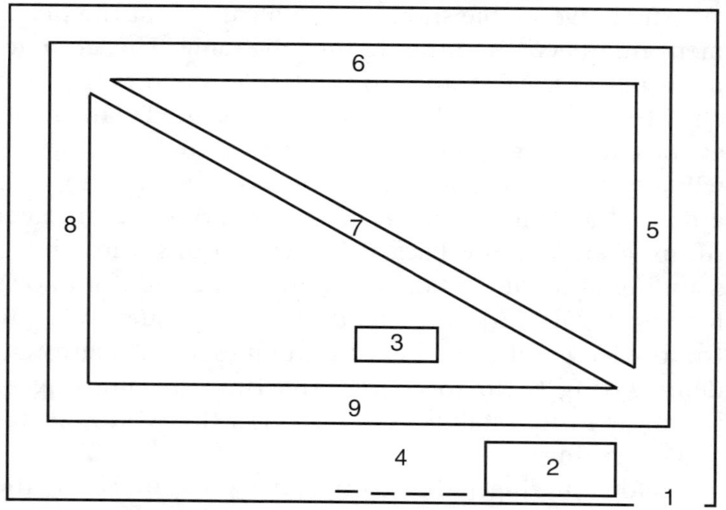

the ring. The most efficient placement is for the diagonal mat to meet the corner where the judge's table is located. This saves the judge from excessive walking from where he does his book work. Outdoor shows do not make use of mats, but the pattern of gaiting would be the same as if there were mats in the ring. In rings in which there are mats, all gaiting should be confined to the mats and no one should be asked to gait a dog across an area not covered by mats.

In rings in which smaller dogs will be shown there will be an examining table. This table should be placed in one of the triangles surrounded by mats. It should be near the point of this triangle where the judge stands while watching a dog gait. It is to the left of the diagonal mat near the long side of the ring where the dogs that are waiting to be examined are standing. This allows each succeeding exhibit to be placed on the table without interrupting the judging of the preceding dog. Before using the table the first time in judging, the judge must determine that the legs are correctly locked and the table will not wobble when a dog is placed on it. If during the course of judging the table is moved, it must be rechecked to see that it is firm and level.

The judge's table is inside the ring and just to the right of the gate. On the table will be the judge's book and the envelope containing the ribbons. There should also be a pitcher of water and glasses, some handiwipes, and paper towels. There may also be trophy cards and, in some cases, the trophies themselves will be in the ring. Anything else should be relegated to the steward's table which is located just outside the ring. The steward's table will hold the armbands, the rubberbands, and the catalogs that the stewards use. These catalogs must not be left so that anyone would believe that the judge could see them if he were so inclined. It must not even appear that this could happen.

The ring stewards are very important in the running of a smooth ring. Good stewards can make the judge look good, and even perhaps better than he really is. The judge should make special note of the stewards' names and probably write them down in case a problem arises at a later date. The steward's marked catalogue may resolve a conflict on absentees or class placements. Many judges ask the inside steward to verify number placements after each class so that any error could be corrected on the spot. It is much easier to correct errors in the judge's book at the time of judging than two or three months later when the Show Records Department of the American Kennel Club writes to question the placement of a specific dog. The superintendent at the show will usually catch errors that are purely mechanical, but he will not be able to find errors of placement. A good ring steward is of great assistance, but a bad one who either has no knowledge of ring procedures or is more interested in chatting with friends at ringside will make the judge's assignment long and taxing.

RING PROCEDURES

Before allowing the steward to call a class of dogs into the ring, the judge must be certain that it is the correct time for that breed to be in the ring. Starting judging before the prepublished time is not permitted and would be a justifiable criticism of the judge. One novice judge at a show moved from one breed to another not noting that there was a time lapse. There had been a number of absentees in the first breed so he finished this judging earlier than expected and moved directly on to the next breed. The ring steward did not notice the error and called the dog in when told to do so. The judge judged the class and finished it before he should have started the breed. An irate exhibitor arrived and protested and the confused judge rejudged the class committing a second error in rejudging a class and changing his book. Because the dog of the late-arriving exhibitor won the second time the class was judged, there was a protest from the original winner.

Once the class is assembled in the ring, the judge must personally check the armbands and should place a check mark in the book in front of the number of each dog present. Some judges allow the ring stewards to do this, which is not the responsibility of the ring steward. This lack of correct ring procedure will be noted on the judge's evaluation sheet if he is observed. Double checking by counting check marks in the book and counting the dogs present in the ring is also a good practice. When starting to judge, the judge must make note of the time the judging started that day.

While the judge is working with his book, the exhibitors have an opportunity to set their dogs up in the most flattering pose since the first impression that the judge receives when he looks at a class is important. A dog that is not properly ring trained will allow its faults to be seen from the very beginning. As the judge walks down the line looking at each dog, he makes mental notes frequently sorting the class into three categories: good, mediocre but promising, and poor. These first impressions will be modified by each successive exercise either as a group or by the individual dog. While these activities will modify the initial impression, it is a vivid one and will be remembered.

While the class go-around does not permit an in-depth examination of any particular dog, it does give an opportunity to switch dogs from one category to another still on a tentative basis. A dog moving too fast or too slow for the normal speed of the group stands out. The cause of this will be determined on the individual gait. This go-around does allow some comparison of the subtleties of gait typical for the breed. It also allows the judge an opportunity to check for lameness of any exhibit.

INDIVIDUAL PHYSICAL EXAMINATION

The individual physical examination of the dog, at least in part, depends on the size of the dog. Large dogs, of course, are examined while standing on the floor, but the smaller breeds are normally examined on the table. Small dogs are examined on the table for several reasons. It is frequently frightening for a small dog to have a very large judge bend down over him and block his view of his handler. It is also easier on both the handler and the judge not to have to get down on the floor to examine a three-pound dog. If the dog is at the approximate waist level of the judge, he can more easily be examined and the judge can see the features he must see clearly and can physically reach all parts of the dog without having to cover him physically with his body during the examination.

There are some breeds that are of a size that can be examined either on the table or on the floor. When there is an option, most judges will select the table. The judge should be consistent and examine each dog in a breed under the same conditions whether it is on the table or on the floor. However, if a dog is frightened on the table and will not stand for examination, the judge has the option to try a second examination on the floor as long as this same courtesy is extended to any other nervous dog. Special care is always exercised when dealing with puppies and novice dogs.

Certain breeds have height and weight disqualifications so special attention must be devoted to these conditions in those particular breeds. A dog that is judged on the table can be measured on the table and can be weighed on the table. Those that are judged on the floor are measured on the floor. The official wicket that is used at shows is very easy to handle. Each leg of the wicket is preset by the judge and the inch number setting on both legs should be shown to the steward and the handler before the judge measures the dog so that there will be no question about the correctness of the number of the setting.

A dog that is to be measured is to be in a correct show pose, one in which the exhibitor would expect the dog to be judged. Many handlers will attempt to pull the dog's head forward and down in an effort to lower the withers and, therefore, the height of the dog. To correct a reluctant handler in properly positioning the dog, the judge may have to tell him that the position in which the dog is measured will be the one in which he will be judged. Once the dog is in a correct show pose and standing near the center of the table, the wicket is brought over the hindquarters of the dog and lowered gently onto the withers. If, when the wicket rests on the withers, both legs do not touch the table, the dog is over the size limit and is disqualified that day. For those breeds which have a minimum height standard, the dog is disqualified if both legs do touch the floor.

Dogs that are judged on the floor are measured on the floor. At inside shows that are on hard surfaces such as concrete or wood, the dog is measured as he stands in a show pose. However, at outdoor shows, or inside shows on dirt or with an uneven surface, a measuring board will be needed. This is a large piece of wood on which the dog can stand comfortably. The board must be stabilized and firm if the dog is to have a fair measurement.

Once a dog has been measured, the judge will have to mark his book indicating that the dog measured outside of the limits for the breed and was disqualified or that he measured within the allowable limits and thus remained in the ring for further consideration.

When a question arises about the weight of a dog in a breed with a weight disqualification, the judge must call for the scales and weigh the dog in the ring. The official scales are easy to use. The predetermined weight is set and shown to the exhibitor, and the dog is then placed on the scale. The balance bar will move when the dog is placed on the scale and the indicator will show whether the dog weighed in or out. The judge will make the appropriate indications in the judge's book and continue with the judging of the class.

Since a number of standards have height and weight limitations, the judge has the obligation to be thoroughly familiar with the use of both the wicket and the scales. It is the judge's responsibility to perform these functions to preserve the breed in the way in which the parent clubs have determined. Some judges are uncomfortable in the use of these instruments and do not measure questionable dogs. They merely place these dogs at the bottom of the class and do not consider them in their placements. This is poor judging and an abrogation of the judge's responsibility.

HANDS-ON EXAMINATION

A thorough hands-on examination is important in any breed since the eye sometimes misinterprets what it is seeing, but the fingers will correct this illusion. With the coated breeds this is an absolute requisite. Some judges only feel certain parts of non-coated dogs and continue the same procedure when they evaluate the coated dogs. In so doing they frequently miss something that should have been noticed. A judge whose basic training was on coated breeds judges with his fingers as much as his eyes, but some judges whose experience was essentially with smooth-coated dogs frequently fail to use their hands correctly when judging the coated breeds. They must learn to use their hands as they grow and mature in their judging.

Since the head fall on some coated breeds may block the judge's view of the eye, the judge should allow the dog to smell his hand before examining him. The judge then proceeds to feel the muzzle, checking for length, shape, and proportions. He then moves to the stop and on to the skull to evaluate shape and size and overall balance with the head as a whole. He then moves on to feel the ears for placement, size, shape, texture, and coloration. The eye is then checked for placement, size, shape, and color. The dentition must be checked to ascertain that it is that which is specified by the standard. Before leaving the head, the judge must check the coat and color pattern if these elements are mentioned in the standard.

Moving from the head down the neck the judge verifies the length, shape, and the joining of the neck to the shoulders. This last element is of extreme importance as it is related to the layback of the forequarters and, therefore, influences the movement of the dog.

The angle of the shoulders in coated dogs must be determined by careful physical examination. The fingers must feel the withers, the point of shoulders, and the placement of the elbows to determine the angulation of the forequarters. The fingers must then remember this angle so it can be compared with the angulation of the hindquarters to determine if the dog is balanced or not. The length of the scapula must be compared to the length of the humerus to ascertain their balance with each other.

Because of the quantity of coat in some breeds, the forelegs must be physically examined from the elbow down to the foot. Some breeds call for a straight front and others allow for a slight curving of the bones of the lower leg. Only a hands-on examination can determine if the dog has what is correct for his breed. Since the feet sometimes cannot be seen, they too must be physically examined to determine their size and shape.

The examination of the body starts from the forechest and proceeds to the pelvis. The forequarters are examined for layback and layto as well as for musculation. The depth and breadth of the rib cage must be felt as well as the length of the back. Next is the coupling and the loin area followed by the pelvis and the croup. The set of the tail as well as its length and quality come next as the logical continuation of the spinal column examination.

In examining the hindquarters, the judge must physically verify the angle between the pelvis and the femur as well as the angle between the femur and the tibia-fibula, and the angle between the tibia-fibula and the metatarsals. The angle between the pelvis and the femur must be compared with that of the scapula-humerus. The wider the divergence of these two angles the greater will be the consequences for the dog when he moves. If the dog is unbalanced, he cannot move with the ease and have the flowing action that he should have.

The angle of the hock and the length of the rear pastern must be determined as well as the shape and size of the hind feet. The hock affects the gait of the dog so it cannot be neglected in the physical examination.

The coat of every breed is an important part of the physical examination as each breed has its own correct type. Since some breeds have such a quantity of coat, it may take just a little longer to examine the coat as it must be checked in several areas. Of most importance is the texture of the coat, both the top coat and the undercoat in breeds that are double coated. Texture is of more importance than either length or quantity. Length and quantity can be the result of grooming techniques, but true texture is natural. Given the great lengths to which exhibitors go in coat preparation, the judge must use great care in checking for foreign substances that might mask or otherwise alter the true texture of the coat. This requires that the judge examine the coat in several areas of the body. He must evaluate the coat of the hindquarters, the back and sides, the forequarters, the head, and the neck. Since most exhibitors do little or nothing to the coat on the inside of the legs because it might interfere with the gait of the dog, the judge should examine this area as possibly being the most substance-free.

The following series of photographs presents a step-by-step technique for the individual physical examination of a dog set up in a show pose on the examining table. The same technique would be used for larger dogs that are examined on the ground. (Below): The judge allows the dog to smell his hand before he starts the examination.

The length of muzzle is measured with the left hand while the right hand holds the head steady.

The length of the skull is measured and then compared for balance with the muzzle according to any ratio established by the standard.

The width of the skull is measured to determine the ratio to the length.

Ear leathers are checked to determine thickness and flexibility and to determine if they have been surgically altered.

Length of neck is measured with a span of fingers.

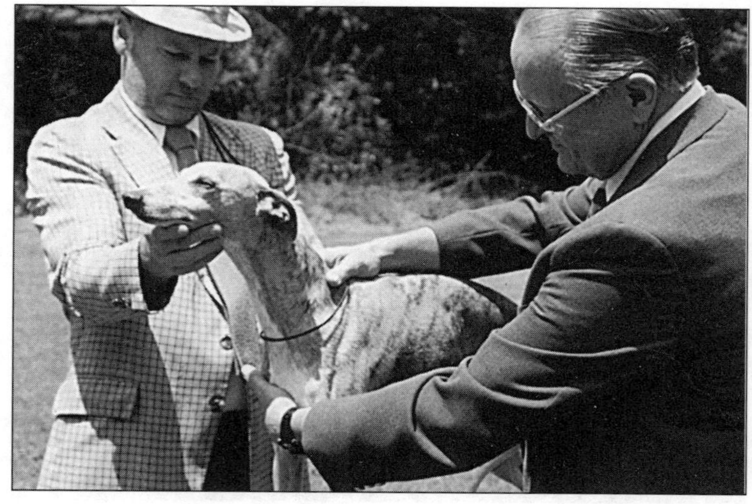

One hand steadies the shoulders while the other hand checks the breadth of chest between the front legs.

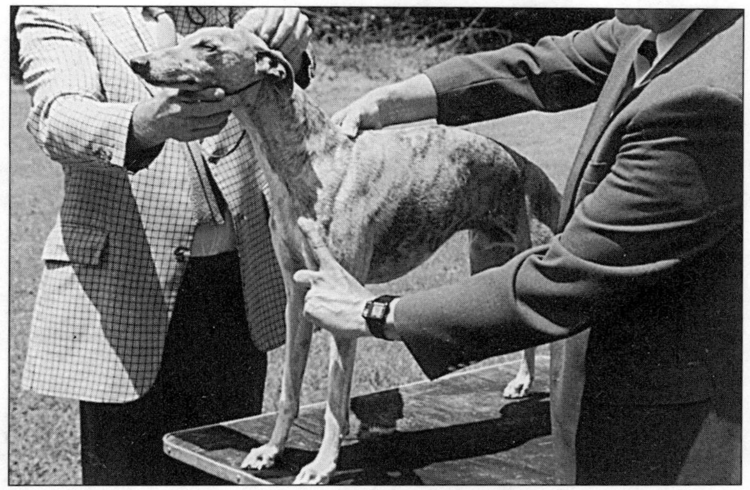

The angulation of the forequarters is verified. One finger is placed on the withers, one finger on the point of shoulder, and another finger on the olecranon at the elbow. In small dogs this can be done with three fingers of one hand. On larger dogs the fingers will slide down the bones as the bones are longer than the span of a hand.

The forearm, carpus, or wrist, and angle of the pastern are determined.

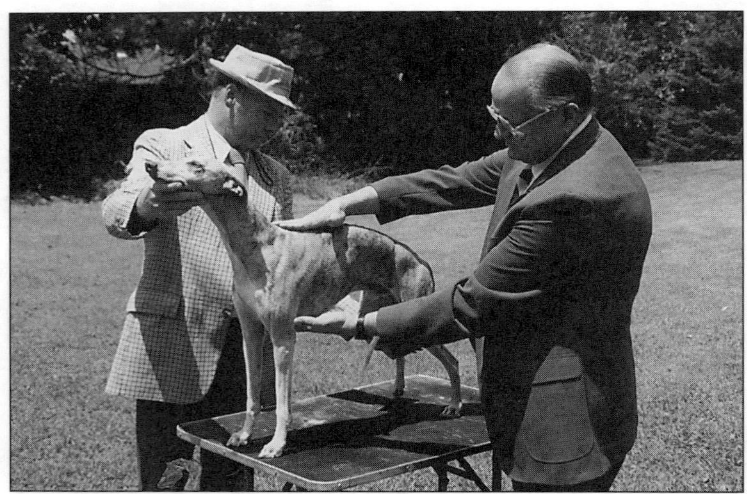

Depth of chest is measured.

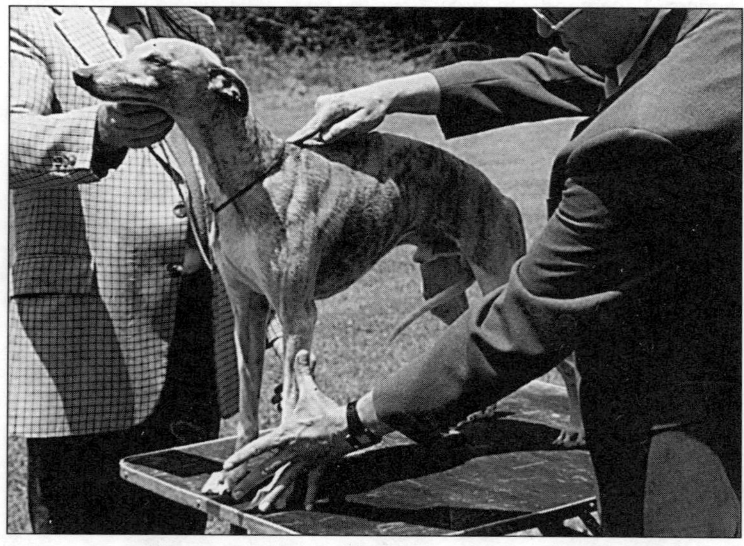

The ratio between the withers to elbow and elbow to ground must be determined when this ratio is expressed in the standard.

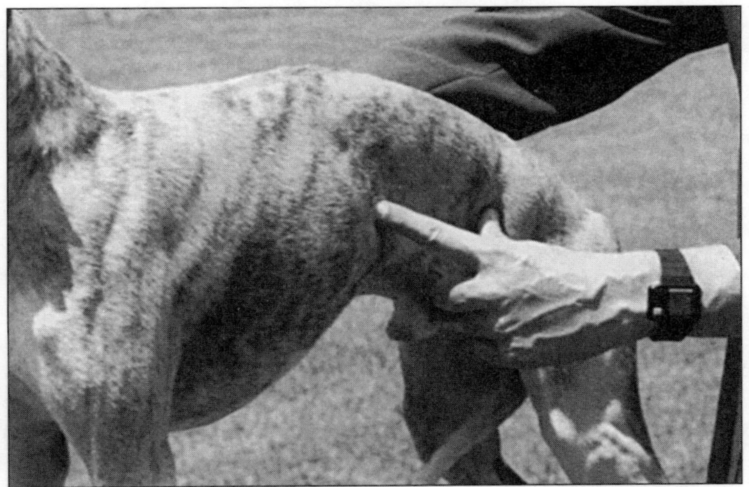

Coupling is determined with one finger on the last rib and another on the front of the thigh.

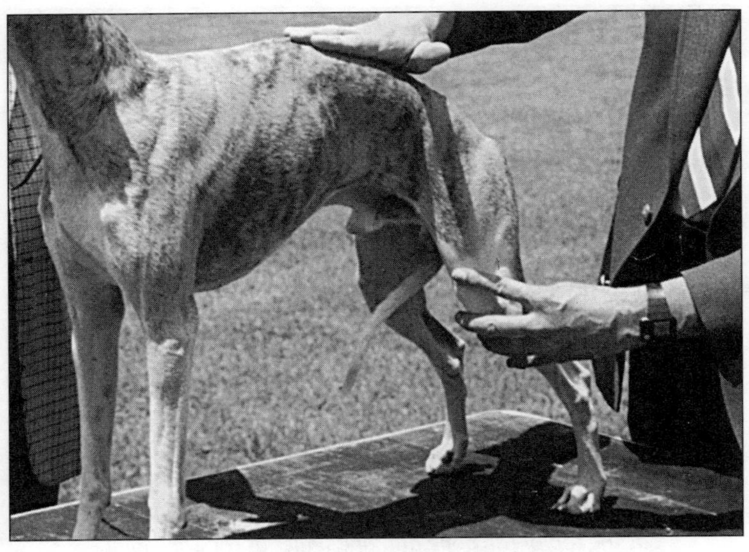

One hand steadies the rear leg while the angle of the croup is measured.

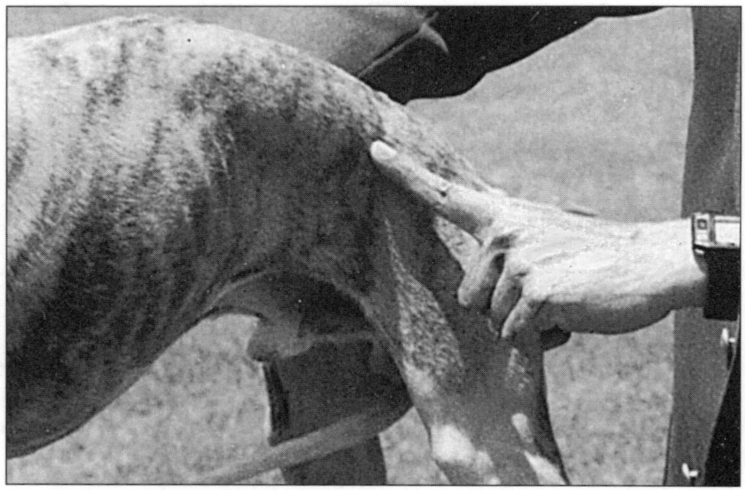

The angle of the pelvis is determined with one finger at the front end of the bone and one finger at the rear end of the bone.

The angle and length of the upper thigh is determined with one finger at the top of the bone and one finger at the stifle joint. The angle where the pelvis and the upper thigh meet is also determined at the same time.

The angle and length of the lower thigh is determined and compared to the length of the upper thigh.

The angle and length of the rear pastern is determined. When the standard says that the hocks are well let down, it means that the rear pastern is short.

The testicles of the males must be checked. This same area in females should be checked to ascertain that a male has not been brought into the ring by mistake.

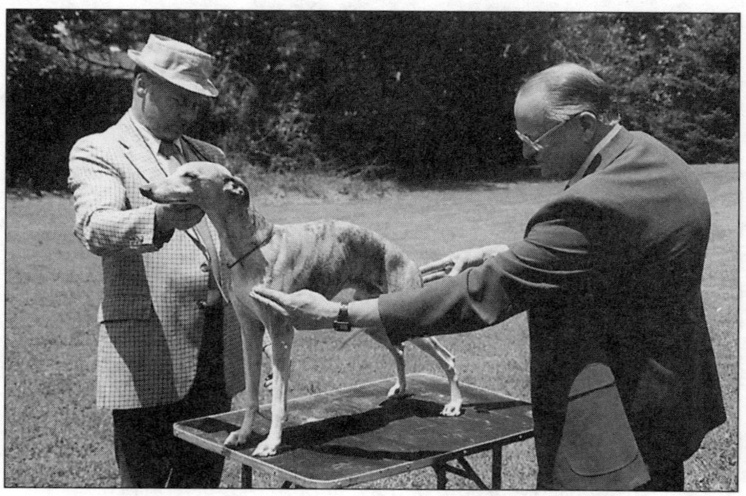

The length of the dog is checked from point of shoulder to the rearmost part of the buttocks.

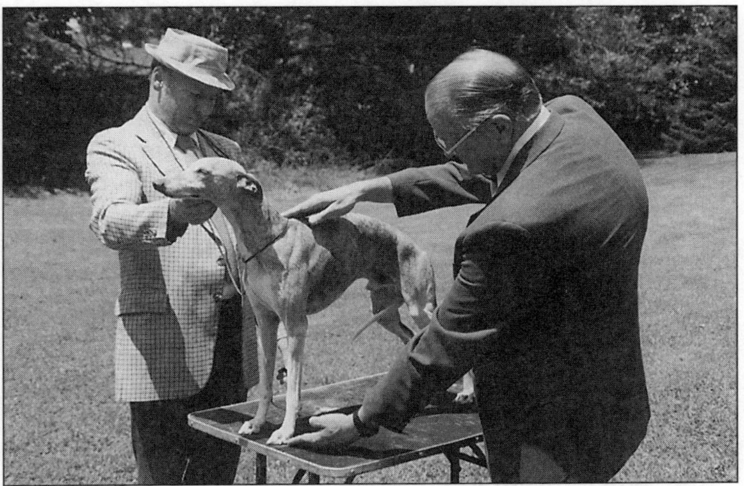

The height of the dog must be determined when the standard lists either an ideal height or has a height disqualification.

GAITING

The last part of the individual examination is the gaiting of the dog. The judge must see the dog going away and coming head on, and must also see the dog move in profile. Probably the most efficient pattern to use is the triangle as the dog's gait is seen from rear, side, and front and the dog does not have to retrace any of his steps. The "L" pattern is frequently used when there is no diagonal mat available or it is blocked by group placement standards. The "T" pattern is sometimes used in group rings when there are three parallel mats. This is probably the least efficient of the three patterns as the end mat which is the top of the "T" is short and the dog does not have an opportunity to move out and demonstrate his side gait.

Gaiting is the final confirmation of the hands-on examination. The results of the physical examination lead the judge to make tentative decisions about the correctness of structure and indicate whether or not the dog will have the typical movement for his breed. The ratio of bone length of the shoulder to the upper arm will affect front movement as will the length of lower arm. The front angulation when compared to rear angulation will indicate whether or not the dog will move straight and true or whether he will crab. The rear angulation is also an important factor in analyzing rear drive. While the physical examination provided the raw data for these tentative decisions, it is the actual gaiting of the dog that gives the confirmation of these decisions.

Most judges feel that the side gait is the single most important aspect in evaluating the gait of the dog. This view allows the judge to see both front and rear quarters at the same time and to evaluate both reach and drive and the balance between the front and the rear quarters of the dog. It has been said that if the side movement is correct, the dog is correctly built. It is easier to see crabbing from either the front or the rear, but it can also be rated by watching the placement of the rear feet as they reach forward. If the dog is overreaching, the rear foot will be placed beside the front foot before it is completely out of the way. When the dog does this, his rear and front will not be tracking on the same plane and one that is parallel to the forward line of motion.

SORTING THE CLASS

Once each individual dog had been examined and gaited, the judge is ready to begin the final selection. During the individual examinations, many judges start making tentative placements so that by the time they have finished the class they already have the class sorted. If the class is unusually large this is not always possible. Whether the placements are made after each dog is examined in a small class of two or three or after the examinations when the large class is reassembled, the sorting process is the same.

The order of priority of the elements of evaluation must be preestablished and should be consistent from class to class and breed to breed. A general priority list for most judges starts with type, which includes general conformation to the standard, gait as it reflects the functional history of the breed, and the temperament, which is also related to function. The dog must first of all be typey or he does not represent the breed. He may have other outstanding qualities and talents, but if he is not typey he cannot be considered as a true representative of the breed.

The elements that are considered after type are balance and soundness, which are closely related. A dog can be very typey, but if he is not balanced between the front and rear quarters he cannot move the way he should. Soundness will also affect the movement of the dog as well as the overall functioning of the animal. A dog can look exactly like the ideal of the breed and be unbalanced and unsound. He can also be balanced and very sound but yet be a very poor representative of the breed. There are a multitude of degrees between these two extremes and it is the judge's responsibility to sort them out and to place the dog which best represents the breed.

This sorting-out process and the individual priority decisions of the judges are what explains the different placements of dogs on consecutive days on a circuit. One judge has remarked that he will put up the most typey dog and disregard soundness and balance as these latter two elements apply to all dogs and do not determine breed type. Another judge just as adamant says that while type is the most important element, it is not the only element to be considered. This judge will place a very typey dog that is unsound below a less typey dog that is more sound. His feeling is that you would not want to include an unsound dog in a breeding program and placing such a dog would endorse this animal as breeding stock. One exhibitor who showed a dog under the first judge and did not win remarked very loudly outside the ring that the judge cared nothing for soundness. This was basically a true statement, but did not take into account the dog's rather obvious lack of type either.

Two other elements to be taken into consideration in evaluating an exhibit are conditioning and showmanship. Some judges will excuse a dog in poor condition that is dirty while other judges will tolerate these exhibits but place them at the end of the line. A dog that is in poor condition, being either too thin or too fat or that is out of coat or has a damaged coat, should not be shown. Dogs that come into the show ring should be properly groomed and conditioned. While this is the responsibility of the exhibitor, it is also the responsibility of the judge to see that the exhibitor knows his obligations and lives up to them.

Showmanship is important since the name of the game is "dog show." If the dog does not show and will not permit a relaxed examination he cannot be honestly evaluated. A dog that cannot be handled and examined should be excused from the ring. However, a dog that is nervous and tense or even shy presents a different problem. Shyness is a fault in some breeds and even more serious in other breeds, calling for dismissal from the ring. There is also the case of the dog of outstanding type that is frightened in the ring and will not carry his tail up and over the back as called for in the standard. This dog is outstanding in quality and in a class with rather poor specimens of the breed who move with their tails up and over as they should. Is the judge justified in putting up this outstanding dog with incorrect tail carriage over the others in the class? Some judges feel that this is correct and that they have the responsibility for putting up type over any other quality. What is the decision if the dog with the tail down is of a little less quality and the other dogs are of a little better quality? This still goes back to the original priority chart of the judge. In the case of the outstanding dog with the tail down, many judges will stop the class and allow the dogs to be set up again and then make the placements when the dog is in a show pose with the tail held up by the handler. It is always the judge's hope that by the time the dog reappears in the winners' class he will have overcome his shyness and will have his tail up.

Showmanship expectations are different from class to class. Most judges will accept lower standards on showmanship with puppies and novice class entries. They would also expect higher levels of showmanship in the special's class. By the time the dog is a champion he should be well schooled in ring procedures. One outstanding dog that was the top winner in his breed was gaiting in the group ring at a show and lost his footing on making a corner. He was really moving too fast and never did recover his composure. He was not placed, much to the dismay of the handler who felt that this error should be forgiven since on other days he never did this. It was pointed out to the handler that the dog is judged each day and not on the collective memory of his performances. The dog is a new dog each day and starts his show career over. Collective memories are for the magazines and the newspapers that advertise dogs and not of importance in the ring itself.

Experienced judges judge faster than new judges and probably the single most important factor that explains this is the priority list of the judge for each of his breeds. He has been judging a breed for some time and has seen all possible combinations of quality and faults and already has their weight and value sorted out and does not have to make these original decisions again at each show.

The new judge, on the other hand, carries the picture of the ideal dog in his mind's eye and knows what he thinks is correct and what he thinks is wrong. His dilemma comes when he looks at a class and finds nothing either completely correct and nothing completely wrong. It is this sorting out of degrees of correctness and incorrectness that takes time. If the judge has potential and a good memory, he will not have to make these exact decisions another day as they will be stored in his memory and he merely has to recall them. Another day will present a different set of degrees of what is correct and what is incorrect and these will also be added to the other stored decisions. While making these decisions in the ring, the novice judge will probably judge at a rate of 20 to 25 dogs per hour. When he gets his priority list well established, he will no longer be a novice and will be judging at a rate of 25 to 28 dogs per hour. While speed of judging should never be a goal of any judge, it is the resulting by-product of experience. There are some judges, unfortunately, who never get beyond the novice category as they remake every decision at every show they judge and never do get their priority list established. These judges will never arrive at the point where they will say, "I have not seen anything new in that breed for years." They will more likely feel that they see new things every time they go into the ring even though they have seen them many times before. These judges never reach the point where they can see these elements in their memory.

DECISION MAKING

Once the class has been individually examined and gaited, the judge must decide whether all dogs in the ring are meritorious and will be placed or whether some of them are non-meritorious and will not be placed. These decisions are at the discretion of the judge and his interpretation of the rules. The judge has the right and, in some cases, the obligation to withhold ribbons and in some cases he may even excuse a dog from the ring. If the judge is a purist and feels a heavy responsibility for maintaining the integrity of the breed, he will take either one or both of these actions depending on the individual quality of the exhibits.

A meritorious dog will be given a placement or at least be considered for a placement in a large class. If, on the other hand, the dog is such a poor representative of the breed that there is even doubt about his origin, he may be excused from the ring with an appropriate indication made in the judge's book. A dog is classified as non-meritorious if he does not resemble the breed. He may also be designated non-meritorious if he has certain faults as spelled out in the standards. Many standards list specific faults while others say that any deviation from the standard is a fault and the degree of this deviation will determine the seriousness of the fault and, therefore, the seriousness of the penalty.

Some breed standards categorize faults as major and minor while other standards classify them as faults, serious faults, and very serious faults. Some standards have excessively long sections dealing with faults and for this reason almost force the judge to fault-judge that breed. While this was undoubtedly not the original intention of the writers of the standard, the detailed divisions and levels of faults must be considered if one is to judge by the standard. If a dog has several serious individual faults and one or two very serious faults, is the judge justified in giving the dog a placement even though he may be a reasonable representative of the breed when considered as a whole? These types of decisions should only have to be made once and then stored in the priority memory bank of the judge.

The decision must be made as to when a ribbon is withheld. Any ribbon may be withheld at any point during the judging. Among the judges that do withhold ribbons there appears to be two schools of thought. One group says withhold the ribbons in the class so that low-quality dogs do not appear in the winners' class. Others say that the placements in the class are merely sorting out that particular group of dogs in relation to one another without thought of awarding points. A second group says that the key to withholding ribbons is in the winners' class since this is where the points are awarded. Both groups are technically correct which permits the judge to make another individual decision and establish his own style.

A dog may be excused from the ring for lack of merit, but he may also be excused for other reasons. If the judge is unable to physically examine a dog, the dog cannot be considered for placement and should be excused from the ring. A dog that allows examination but refuses to gait can also be excused from the ring, although some judges will simply place this dog at the end of the line in the hopes that he may gait when the entire class starts to move. Sometimes they do and sometimes they do not. If this dog is at the end of the line, he is at least not interfering with the other dogs and the judge has had an opportunity to evaluate his conformation. A dog that limps must be excused from the ring. In the past the veterinarian was called to determine if the dog was limping, but now this responsibility is assigned to the judge. Ringside spectators can see when a dog is limping, and when the judge does not excuse this dog, it is evident for all to see and be remembered.

A number of standards list disqualifications. Disqualifications leave nothing to the judge's discretion or interpretation. A dog with a disqualifying fault must be dismissed from the ring with the appropriate notation made in the judge's book. Height and weight disqualifications are easy to verify and it is the judge's obligation to weigh and measure when there is a borderline animal in the ring. Merely not considering this dog for a placement is not fair to the dog or to the exhibitor. If the dog is close to the limit but would be within limits, measuring and weighing will eliminate doubt and allow the dog to be considered.

Disqualifications for faults other than height and weight are also usually very specific and easy to determine. The Kerry Blue Terrier standard calls for the dog to be disqualified if there are dewclaws on the rear legs. This is an unusual disqualification since it can so easily be corrected. A dog can be disqualified one day, have the dewclaws removed and be back in the ring the next weekend. It would seem that disqualifications should be designated for serious genetic faults rather than for something that can easily be corrected.

Since viciousness and shyness have been long-standing problems in some breeds, these disqualifications address a serious condition in the breed. Since missing teeth and being overshot or undershot could well interfere with the working of a dog, this disqualification also addresses a need in the breed. Other disqualifications such as coat, or coat color, or coat pattern are more cosmetic, but they usually have some historical significance in the development of the breed.

Disqualifications were established by parent clubs for a variety of reasons, some of which may be less valid today than in the past. However, no matter the reason for the disqualification, if it exists in the standard it must be looked for and if found the dog must be dismissed from the ring. This is the judge's responsibility, and no matter what his personal preferences may be, he must apply the rule. If this means measuring out a dog in the Group or Best-in-Show ring, so be it. An oversized dog in the Group ring means that the breed judge failed in his obligations to the sport. If the Group judge also ignores the situation, it only complicates the situation. Most regular exhibitors in a breed know when a dog is oversized or undersized, and a judge that ignores the rules does not gain respect, but indicates to the exhibitor that this is the person to whom to bring any oversized or undersized dogs that they may have. One handler, when asked about the dogs she brought to certain judges, said, "I bring garbage dogs to garbage judges." Staying out of the garbage should be the goal of every judge.

Handlers of winning dogs frequently request that a photograph be taken either to be used as a record of the win, or so that it can be used in advertising, or so they can have an opportunity to talk to the judge and comment on the great qualities of his dog just in case the judge might have missed them. If there are a number of breeds being judged during one hour, it is somewhat more efficient to hold all photographs until the hour assignment is over. If all judges follow the same procedure, however, this plan will not work and it might be more efficient to take all pictures halfway through the hour.

PLACEMENTS

It is usually best not to place dogs while they are on the move as this sometimes leads to confusion as to just which dog had which placement since judge and handler eye contact may have been lost. Some judges feel that placing dogs on the move is more dramatic and prefer to do this. If this is the case, the dogs should be placed in line in the same order in which they will finally be placed before the last go-around so there will be no possible confusion in anyone's mind as to which dog won which placement.

If the class is large there will be four placements, while in smaller classes there may be only one or two ribbons given out. The blue ribbon is for first place, the red for second, the yellow for third, and the white for fourth place.

After each class is judged, the first place winners from each class are called back to compete in winners' class. As these class winners come back into the ring, the judge must recheck each armband to make sure that the correct dogs are in the ring. An exhibitor with several entries may return with the wrong armband or even the wrong dog if he is hurrying too much. These errors should be caught before the class is judged and not wait until the dogs are placed. In the case in which the blue ribbon was withheld in a class, there will be no representative from that class. The winner of the winners' class will be designated as winner's dog or winner's bitch and will receive a purple ribbon. The dog that placed second in the original class from which the winner's dog or winner's bitch came will return to the ring to compete for reserve winners. The winner of this class receives a purple and white ribbon. There is a special case involving a dog that was double-entered in two classes. He won one class and came in second in the other. Since he was already defeated by another dog he cannot compete in the winners' class, but if the winner's dog was the only dog that defeated him, he may return to the ring for reserve winners.

Breed competition is limited to champions, winner's dog and winner's bitch, and in some cases the winner of the veteran dog and veteran bitch classes. From this class is selected the Best of Breed, the Best of Winners, and the Best of Opposite Sex, in that order. An error that is seen occasionally is when a judge places as Best of Opposite Sex a dog of the same sex as the Best of Breed. If the judge does not catch his own error, he must hope that the exhibitor will point the error out to him. If the error is not caught in the ring, either the superintendent or the American Kennel Club will eventually discover it and the judge will have to explain what happened. The Best of Winners will either be the winner's dog or the winner's bitch as no other dog is eligible for this win. In the case where there was only either a winner's dog or a winner's bitch there can be no Best of Winners. The Best of Breed receives a purple and yellow ribbon, the Best of Winners receives the blue and white ribbon, and the Best of Opposite Sex receives the red and white ribbon.

Some shows offer non-regular classes which might include a Local Dog class, Brace and Team competition, Brood Dog and Brood Bitch, or Veteran Dog and Veteran Bitch. With the exception of Veteran Dog and Veteran Bitch, which are eligible for Best-of-Breed competition, these non-regular classes are judged after the Best of Breed is awarded.

The Best-of-Breed winner from each breed competes for one of the four placements in the Group, and the winners of the seven Groups compete for Best in Show. The Best-in-Show ribbon is red, white, and blue.

After each class, the judge must mark his judge's book indicating the placements. The placement number is placed after the armband number of the winning dog. The safest policy for a judge to follow is to check each armband as he gives out each ribbon. Eager stewards are always willing to call out the armband numbers, but if there is an error, it is the judge's and not the ring steward's and the judge is the person who must explain it at a later date, sometimes months after the show when the Show Records Department of the American Kennel Club is notified by an exhibitor that an error has been published in the Gazette. It is difficult to correct these records after such a time lapse. Since ring stewards also mark their books, some judges ask the steward to verify his markings for one class while he is judging the next class. This way an error is caught immediately and easily corrected while everyone is still present. One common error that appears from time to time is marking down the number of the armband rather than the number of the placement. If only one such error is made in a class it is easy to correct, but if two or more of these errors are made in one class the steward's book can be very helpful. The best advice that can be offered is to concentrate on numbers when marking the book and check them again as the exhibitors leave the ring.

CRITIQUES

Breed clubs frequently ask judges to give either an oral report of the judging or to write an article for the breed magazine. This is standard procedure at most shows abroad, but is rather the exception in the United States. Occasionally a judge will be asked to make some sort of statement for the television cameras as is seen after the Westminster Kennel Club show. Judges should expect such requests and be prepared to honor them.

Oral reports are usually given at the banquets following specialty shows. Judges normally confine their remarks to general observations on the improvement of the breed during recent years but will occasionally mention specific faults that might have been detected during the day's judging without making reference to any particular class or dog. Breeder judges will usually be much more specific than generalists, but this is not always the case. Remarks about individual dogs are saved for the top winners of the day: Best of Breed, Best of Opposite Sex, winner's dog, and winner's bitch. These remarks are limited to the outstanding qualities of breed type and overall quality. Negative statements are not made in a public forum.

Written reports are submitted to the club bulletin to be published at a later date. In these cases the judge will frequently comment about specific placements in the classes as well as offer more general remarks about the overall quality of the entry at the show. Any negative remarks about problems are of a most general nature without making reference to any particular dog or even class. Exhibitors want to hear and read the good things but generally do not want problems aired publicly. The remarks that the judge makes after the show can be compared to the usher's bringing flowers to the star of a play after the play is over. The audience wants only to see the flowers and not hear the criticism.

It is to be remembered that the judge's placements at the show are already a statement of his thoughts about quality or lack thereof of the entries at the show. Knowledgeable exhibitors already know what strengths and weaknesses the judge has found and what his relative ratings in these areas are. This is true when there is a large entry, but when the entire show is small this may be somewhat more difficult to interpret.

While neither oral nor written reports are the general rule at present, they are occasionally requested and each judge should be prepared to provide such when asked. One way to facilitate this task is to make short notes after each class at a specialty show so that the judge will not have to rely on his memory afterwards. Notes can be very brief and even in the judge's special code to save time. When the judge finishes writing the notes he should cover them since exhibitors at ringside will try to read what he has written once he has left the table. If the notes contain any negative comments, this could prove to be embarrassing. Some judges dictate into tape recorders, which saves time and can be transcribed later.

COURTESY LETTERS

Some judges write thank-you notes to the clubs after they have judged their shows. While this practice was very common in the past, it is less so today. It is still considered a polite gesture and a wise practice for new judges at the beginning of their careers.

Self-Test Questions

1. Who has the final authority in the ring?
2. What are common ring size measurements?
3. How important are good stewards?
4. Where should placement markers be in relation to the judge's table?
5. Why should the judge walk around his ring before the start of judging?
6. What must be checked on the examining table?
7. In divided classes, how many dogs should be held from the first division?
8. Why must the judge personally check each armband number?
9. How does the judge indicate that a dog was present for judging?
10. What is the value of the original setup?
11. Must each dog in a class be examined in the same way?
12. When are dogs measured on the table?

Self-Test Questions

13 What does the expression "seeing with the fingers" mean?

14. Why is the examination of the hock important?

15. What is the most important quality of coat?

16. Where is the most substance-free area of the dog?

17. Which is the most efficient gaiting pattern?

18. Which is the least satisfactory gaiting pattern?

19. Which view of the dog gaiting is most important?

20. Which is the more important, type or soundness?

21. Why are placements different from day to day on a dog show circuit?

22. What should the judge do with a dog that will not stand for examination?

23. Why can experienced judges judge faster than new judges?

24. Which ribbons may be withheld for lack of merit?

25. Must a limping dog be excused from the ring?

26. What are the most common types of disqualifications?

Evaluating Judging Ability

The decision to elect a career as a dog show judge requires a relatively high level of self-confidence and knowledge sufficient to be able to make decisions quickly and correctly under the pressures present in the ring. Those who do not have self-confidence and breed knowledge would be ill-advised to undertake such an occupation. While these two elements are extremely important in the initial decision to become a judge, they are only part of the overall elements needed to maintain a career as a judge.

Judging requires a regimen of continuing education and self-evaluation if one expects to be successful and have the respect of the exhibitors and the breeders. Exhibiting dogs is an expensive hobby and the exhibitor has every right to expect that he is receiving honest and knowledgeable evaluations of his dogs. Those individuals who are not willing to undertake continuing education and evaluation would be well advised not to apply for judging privileges. Judging is not for everyone in the dog world since it requires different talents and abilities from the breeder and the exhibitor. It is an area in which decision making leads to challenges on a daily basis. When exhibitors are displeased with a judge's decision they may question it verbally or through body language. These challenges are more frequent at the beginning of a judge's career than they are later on when the judge has an established reputation and knowledgeable exhibitors know exactly what type of dog to bring him. In the beginning the pattern has not as yet been set so exhibitors do not know exactly what to expect.

A judge's most severe critic should be the judge himself. He should be the most difficult person to satisfy since he is solely responsible for the initial decision to become a judge and for the continuing decision to persevere in judging. He alone knows whether or not his decisions in the ring are based solely on the quality of the exhibit or have been colored by some other extraneous element. Personal integrity should be foremost in the mind of the judge at every show. Once a tainted decision has been made, the judge has compromised his career. A conscious decision to place a dog on something other than the individual merits of the dog is different from a mistake made by having missed some element in the examination of the dog. The careless error, while unjustifiable, is of a different nature than the conscious one.

SELF-EVALUATION

There will be many different kinds of critics and evaluators in a judge's career, but they will not have the advantage of the inside information that the judge has of the elements that resulted in the final decision making. Self-evaluation is a continuous and on-going process. It is on-going in that it should occur even during the judging process itself. The judge needs to have active recall of other assignments in the same breed and ascertain that he is using the same standards that he used the last time. If, however, some new element or quality is found in a dog then the decision-making process must, of course, be modified. Short of this new element, however, the same rules and their application should result in the placement of the same type of dog for the same reasons. As judges gain more ring experience and learn more about each breed over the years, they may consciously or unconsciously change their

One way for a judge to study his ring procedures is to have his judging videotaped for later viewing.

concept of the ideal breed type. This, however, is an evolutionary process that goes on over a period of years and could be easily followed by the longtime exhibitor who has watched a judge grow in knowledge. Changes should not take place on a weekly basis because that would leave everyone confused as to exactly what a particular judge considers the ideal dog in a breed.

The self-evaluation starts when the judge watches the dogs go around the ring for the first time. He should be looking only at the dogs and should be looking for typical gait and breed outline and making tentative decisions as to which dogs have these qualities and which do not. If the judge is not intent on this process, he may be distracted by some element which has nothing to do with the decision-making process. If each dog is not examined in the same way and in the same sequence, the judge has made a small error. Since exhibitors are supposed to watch the way the judge makes his examinations and decisions, changing the procedure only leads to confusion and possible criticism. There are exceptions that can be made from time to time depending on circumstances. When a small dog will not tolerate being examined on the table, the judge, after trying on the table, may try to examine the dog on the floor. This is acceptable so long as the same courtesy is extended to any other nervous dog.

Serious judges still review the standards of the breeds they will be judging the night before the show. The judge with only one or two breeds is also well advised to adopt this policy. Multi-breed judges who may not have judged a certain breed for a period of weeks definitely do need to review the standard before undertaking the assignment. Active recall of a particular standard may become confused with the standard of another similar breed if it is not reviewed on a regular basis. Some judges make special cards on individual breeds with key information concerning that breed which they use to refresh their memory while in the ring. A number of breed standards list three or four elements that are peculiar to that breed and truly define type. Breed videos are even more specific on these special qualities.

Judges sometimes experience surprise when a dog they have given winner's returns for breed competition and looks entirely different. This is the result of the fact that the original handler has handed the dog off to someone else so that he can bring in a special or so he can take a different dog into another ring. When the first handler was extremely talented and thoroughly understood the dog and his faults, he was able to present the dog in the most favorable aspect. The second handler does not have the same degree of talent or knowledge of the dog and cannot mask the faults and show the dog to his best advantage. When this is obvious, the judge must ask himself whether or not he evaluated the dog to the best of his ability the first time. When the dog looks very different, the answer to that question is probably that the judge did not do his best job with the original placement. The handler has the responsibility to present the dog in the best possible light minimizing the faults and emphasizing the good qualities. It is the judge's responsibility to credit the good qualities and to find and honestly evaluate the faults and then weigh one against the other. When the faults of a dog do not appear until after the dog has earned the winner's ribbon, the judge appears to have failed somewhat in his original decision. There may be extenuating circumstances in some cases, but in every such case the judge truly needs to review his examination procedures and his decision-making process.

Post-ring self-evaluation is also an important element of a day's judging assignment. After breed judging or even later in the day, the judge needs to rethink the decisions he made that day. When the judge is doing the group of the breeds he did that day, he automatically does this in anticipation of the exhibits he will have back in the group ring at the end of the day. He sorts these dogs out and re-evaluates each breed winner comparing the winner of the day to the outstanding dog he holds in his mind's eye. Some judges use a ten-point scale, awarding a ten to the dog that they consider ideal for the breed. The dog they had on the current day of judging may be only a four by comparison and, therefore, it will be defeated in the group by any dog who has received a five or higher rating. For judges who work regularly with such a system it is easy and efficient. There are many other individual systems for comparing oranges and apples and each judge should select the one that works the best for him as long as he can justify it and be consistent with its application. No matter what system is used the judge must regularly ask himself, "Did I do it right? Was I fair and impartial?" These questions are automatic self-evaluators.

Rethinking the placements of the day allows the judge to evaluate any decision that was close between two different dogs. While time limitations require prompt decisions in the ring, reconsidering the process later allows a more leisurely analysis and an opportunity to establish for subsequent assignments some way to facilitate a similar decision when the facts are the same.

PEER EVALUATION

Judges who have self-confidence are always willing to ask other more experienced and breed-knowledgeable judges for advice. Any judge who is reluctant to ask for help needs to re-examine this lack of confidence. The dedicated judge should never fear to expand his knowledge nor should he consider this as evidence that he is less than qualified because of it. Multi-group judges frequently can be heard asking long-time breeders questions about specific points of a breed. This certainly does not demonstrate a lack of knowledge on the part of the judge, but rather a desire to be a better judge.

Dedicated judges still consult with individuals who are involved in a breed of which the judge was originally a breeder. Since styles and goals change over the years, the judge may want to obtain new information as well as to share his own knowledge. Sharing and seeking knowledge are merely different approaches to the same goal.

A judge who has been judging a breed for a number of years may want to consult another judge about some aspect of a particular dog to get his reaction to it. This frequently happens when some new quality or problem begins to appear in a breed because of changing fashions. While it may appear that some breeders are causing these changes and others are tolerating them, it is the judge's responsibility to judge by the standard and to keep the breed as pure as possible and historically correct according to the standard. Consultation with other judges can either reinforce this knowledge or correct it if it is in error.

When a judge is passing on newly acquired breeds for the first few times, he frequently consults with more experienced judges after he has done an assignment. By the time a judge reaches the point where he will have his first assignment in a new breed, he will have examined individual dogs, is thoroughly familiar with the standard, and if he has studied the breed books, examined numerous individual specimens outside the ring, and watched the breed videos, he knows exactly what he considers the ideal for that breed. However, when he goes into the ring for the first assignment in a new breed and does not find what he considers ideal or even correct, he begins slowly to compare the individual dogs in the ring to his ideal dog and rates them as to how closely they approach this ideal. Some breeds seem to have two or three distinct variations of type and the judge must make the determination as to what he considers correct and then be consistent in his placements. Days when such a situation occurs lead a judge to seek help from a more experienced colleague. A judge will sometimes ask another judge in the next ring to watch his judging of a new breed if there is an opportunity. This allows for a serious consultation later in the day and both judges can discuss individual dogs based on similar knowledge. The actual judge will have the hands-on knowledge, but there can still be a good exchange of information.

AMERICAN KENNEL CLUB EVALUATION

The American Kennel Club continually evaluates all judges. This is done at three different levels. The basic evaluation is performed by the Field Representatives at the shows. The Field Representative will sit ringside and watch a judge do one or more breed assignments. He will make notes and later in the day will prepare a written evaluation of the judge's performance on that day. This evaluation will be presented to the judge at the end of the day and the judge will be asked to sign the report to indicate that he has in fact received a copy of the report. His signature does not indicate that he agrees with the report, but merely indicates that he has read the report and has received a copy.

When the Field Representative gives the report to the judge, he will discuss any deficiencies that have been noted and make suggestions as to how these deficiencies can be corrected. If regular negative reports are filed on a judge, that judge needs to undertake a serious self-evaluation as to his goals and objectives, and even to question his continuing as a judge. Field reports for the most part deal with ring procedures and mechanics and do not evaluate the placements per se of individual dogs. A judge who is not in control of his ring and cannot operate in an efficient and professional manner needs to make major changes in his approach to judging. Every exhibitor has the right to expect a high degree of professionalism in the ring. He should not expect to win at every show, but he can expect thorough and professional treatment and a knowledgeable and fair evaluation of his dog.

Field Representative reports are filed in Judges Department at the American Kennel Club and become a permanent part of the judge's file. These reports are reviewed by the staff from time to time and are thoroughly reviewed when a judge applies for additional breeds. These reports are considered by the Staff Committee as it makes its recommendations to the Board of Directors on an application.

This evaluation is then forwarded to the Board of Directors for its final decision and disposition of the application for additional breeds. This review of the judge's file is in fact a formal evaluation of the judging ability of the individual judge. If the evaluation is negative and the application is disapproved, an appeal can be made and the judge has an opportunity to appear personally before the Committee for review. The appeals process is explained in the *Guidelines for Dog Show Judges*.

EXHIBITOR EVALUATION

While exhibitor evaluation of the judge may be either positive or negative, it is usually on the negative side. Positive evaluation, for the most part, consists of a "Thank you" for a ribbon, especially if it is a first or higher award. The lower the placement, the less enthusiastic the "Thank you."

When an exhibitor does not win and speaks to a judge about the placement of his dog, he usually does not want to hear an explanation from the judge even though this is what he is requesting. He usually wants an opportunity to tell the judge what a fine dog he had that day and indicate to the judge that the evaluations were less than correct under this judge. These exhibitors usually do not listen when the judge tries to explain why a particular dog was given a certain award on that day. Novice exhibitors may be an exception to this in that they are really trying to find out if the placement was entirely on the quality of the dog or partly on the lack of quality of their handling which might have prevented the judge from fairly evaluating the dog. Novice exhibitors deserve detailed and thoughtful explanations in terms they can understand. They also need suggestions on presentation and grooming in some cases. Time needs to be set aside to assist these individuals at the beginning of what may turn out to be a long career of exhibiting dogs. Even if it turns out to be a short career, they deserve this treatment.

Long-established breeders who have shown to a judge over a period of years sometimes express concern to a judge when they feel that he has placed a dog that is different from the type of dog he normally puts up. This concern is usually expressed in a constructive and positive way. When the comment is offered in this fashion it can be a very valuable learning experience for the judge. This concern offers an opportunity for an exchange of ideas that will be beneficial for both parties.

There are other times, however, when an exhibitor manifests a negative and hostile approach to a judge while questioning a decision about the placement of a particular dog. A conversation between two hostile individuals produces heat but no light. It is most definitely to the judge's advantage to remain calm and cool and to listen to the complaint from the exhibitor. Being calm and cool allows for an impartial evaluation of the exhibitor's remarks. They may contain some worthwhile information which should be accepted. If, on the other hand, they are prejudiced and vindictive it is another matter. It is difficult to listen to these remarks when such remarks are not complimentary to the judge. The exhibitor wants to be heard and if the judge keeps interrupting him he will only become more frustrated. If he is not interrupted, he will shortly run out of steam and things to say and he will begin repeating himself which he will shortly realize. The hostile complainer expects to be interrupted by the judge as he tries to justify himself and this only adds to the anger and energy of the complainer. When no hostility is returned by the judge, the hostile exhibitor is frequently put off. One judge who never attempts to justify a decision in the face of open hostility merely says: "Thank you for this exchange of opinions. I will certainly think over your comments." This really does not leave the exhibitor any place to go but away. He will be somewhat satisfied in that he got to say what he intended, but may also feel cheated that he did not get to mount a new attack since the judge did not try to justify himself.

Some judges become angry in the face of hostile exhibitors and may even surpass the exhibitor in hostility.

This usually does not produce a reasonable solution as there can be no satisfaction on either side. Since dog showing is a sport of gentlemen, hostility has no place in the arena. A cooling-off period should most certainly precede such conversations rather than following them.

If an exhibitor gets out of control and will not break off what amounts to an attack on the integrity of the judge, the only solution left for the judge is to call for a Bench Show Committee Hearing. This should be done promptly by summoning the Bench Show Committee Chairman who will convene the committee hearing. Most hostile exhibitors, or at least their friends, will intervene before the situation reaches this extreme, but when they do not the Bench Show Hearing is the only solution. The American Kennel Club has prepared a brochure governing Bench Show Hearings which every judge should read. It is also advisable for the judge to carry this brochure in the folder with his standards in case a question comes up at a show.

It is the responsibility of the judge to make every effort to maintain a smooth-running ring and to make thoughtful and consistent decisions. When this process breaks down, it is still the responsibility of the judge to maintain the decorum of the dog show. If this means assembling a Bench Show Hearing, this is also part of the judge's responsibility.

Letters of complaint against a judge are occasionally filed with the American Kennel Club and become a permanent part of the judge's file. These letters could be signed or anonymous. Starting in 1989, a judge may obtain copies of any letters received by the American Kennel Club regarding his judging competence. Xerox copies are supplied to the judge upon request. There has been a marked decline in such letters since the complainer knows that the judge will receive a copy of the signed letter. Anonymous letters are destroyed upon receipt by the

American Kennel Club and do not become a part of the judge's file.

The judge is obligated to listen to expressions of concern on the part of exhibitors and to offer explanations when this is appropriate and there is evidence that the exhibitor will listen to such explanations. When there is every indication that the exhibitor is so hostile that explanations will not satisfy, he needs to resolve the situation in the most efficient and quiet manner possible. No matter how distasteful it may be, the situation must be resolved. Whether it means merely walking away or calling a Bench Show Committee Hearing, there is always some solution. Reviewing the situation later may offer greater insight should a similar situation arise at a future show.

Everyone cannot win at a given show so everyone cannot be equally happy. The most and the least that an exhibitor should expect is that he have fair, consistent, and impartial consideration from a knowledgeable judge.

Self-Test Questions

1. Who should be the judge's most severe critic?
2. When should a judge change his decision-making process?
3. When does the self-evaluation process begin in judging a breed?
4. When should standards be reviewed?
5. Should a judge consult the standard in the ring?
6. What is the ten-point ideal breed dog system?
7. What are two self-evaluation questions?
8. When should one judge consult another judge or a long-time breeder about a problem of breed interpretation?
9. What does the American Kennel Club Field Representative's report cover?
10. When should a Bench Show Committee Hearing be called?
11. What does judging require if you expect to be successful at it?
12. What purpose does post-ring self-evaluation serve?
13. Why is peer evaluation important in your judging education?

Judging Junior Showmanship is another phase of exhibitor education. It helps to set a standard for the next generation of handlers.

Scheduling Assignments

It is important that a judge keep accurate records of all his assignments to avoid any possible conflicts in breed assignments. The American Kennel Club rule states that, in order to avoid overexposure, a judge may not judge a breed twice within thirty days within a radius of two hundred miles. This rule protects the exhibitor from showing the same dog to the same judge at too close an interval of time. It is probably wise for the judge not to accept assignments at an even longer interval in the same general area as his entries would undoubtedly drop. Certain kennel clubs, especially in the southwest and on the west coast, put additional limitations on this time-distance restriction. Some clubs extend the distance limit to four hundred miles and some set time limits of either four or six months. National breed clubs frequently impose six-month limits on judging that breed anywhere in the United States. This limitation poses few problems for the multi-group judge, but would be a more serious restriction for the limited breed judge. However, the opportunity to do a national specialty in most cases would offset these limitations. Regional and local breed clubs may also impose some special limitations but these are usually less restrictive. These extended limitations are within the rights of a show-giving club, and if a judge disapproves of such restrictions, he does not have to accept the assignment. The greatest difficulty that results from these extended limits is that the clubs do not make assignments at the time of hiring and state that the specific breed assignments will follow shortly. Sometimes they do and sometimes they do not. When the delays are long, many judges give priority to the first breed-specific assignments and let late-filing clubs sort out the problems if any arise. Clubs would be well advised to make specific assignments within a month of the original contract. There is no reason they cannot do this and it would greatly reduce conflicts for all concerned.

In the past most original contacts between judges and clubs were arranged by letter in a very formal manner. Currently most clubs make the initial contact by telephone as this is much more efficient. If the show chairman has his panel tentatively in place and the judge is available and the fee acceptable, a commitment can be made at the time of the original contact. If the show chairman is truly efficient, he will also have his breed assignments worked out and can put a tentative hold on them. Most judges will inform the contact that they will put a tentative hold on a show date for a period of one month or even six weeks. They will hold that date for that period of time in order to receive a written contract. This policy makes it important for the judge to date his notes about the show and also include the name of the contact person and that person's telephone number. If the formal contract is not received within the reserved time period, the judge is free to accept another assignment on that date. As a courtesy to the original club, the judge should contact the show chairman either to establish the status of the contract or to inform him that he is no longer holding the date.

JUDGING FEES

There seems to be no accepted structure for the establishment of the fees that a judge charges a club. The judge states what his charge will be to the club for his services, and the club either accepts or rejects the offer of the judge. Limited breed judges who are approved for fewer breeds than an entire group usually judge on a per-dog fee for their services. A few years ago this fee was one dollar per dog, but at present the going market price appears to be three to four dollars for each dog entered under that judge. Clubs can afford to hire limited breed judges at this cost, and the limited breed judge does receive some help with his expenses and has an opportunity to judge which he might otherwise not receive if he were to charge the club a higher rate.

Group judges operate under a different set of rules. With rare exception, they all charge at least their expenses. If they are delegates to the American Kennel Club, this is all that they are allowed to charge for their services. A number of clubs take advantage of the service of those judges who are delegates as it helps to keep the cost of a panel lower than it would be otherwise. Some judges charge their out-of-pocket expenses plus a fee. Fees range from as little as fifty dollars to as much as five hundred dollars. A rule of thumb that some clubs use is that they will allow a fee of one hundred dollars for a judge with one group and an additional fifty dollars for each additional group since the multi-group judge does give greater flexibility to the panel and helps with last minute overloads. Most clubs have a maximum limit on the fee that they will pay a judge. If a judge charges over this maximum, they will simply not hire that judge.

RECORD KEEPING

Accurate record keeping is of great importance both to the judge and to the show-giving club. If a judge has held a date for a club and subsequently finds he is not on the panel when he has turned down additional assignments on that date, he is frustrated. The same is true from the point of view of the club when it has counted on the services of a particular judge only to find that he had accepted another assignment for their date. If this judge's assignment had been spread over several groups, it makes it even more difficult to find specific breed replacements.

There are many different methods of keeping accurate records that are easy to read and that facilitate rapid reference. One of these is the slot file, which is similar to the card files used beside time clocks for hourly workers. The cards in these slots can display at a glance the date and locations of a show on the top portion of the card. The bottom of the card in the slot can contain the breed assignments. Since both date and location information is visible at a glance it is very easy to check for possible distance-time conflicts since it is only necessary to look at the preceding and following few cards. Each slot can cover a single weekend with cluster shows on the same card.

While the slot card file is efficient for quick reference, it cannot hold the correspondence for the shows. There are a number of methods of handling this correspondence. One system is a loose-leaf notebook which includes dividing sheets for each month so that correspondence can be kept in chronological order. This notebook reference is easy to use as things can be added and removed quickly. A single notebook can accommodate files for three separate years even for a very active judge.

Another useful device for keeping correspondence organized is the pocket portfolio which is divided into twelve monthly sections. This is an easy-to-use item but does require a separate portfolio for each year. Also available commercially is a five-year booklet divided into months. Correspondence can be filed in the appropriate section but as the book is bound it does not allow for the necessary expansion.

One of the new electronic devices that can readily be used by judges to keep show information with them at all times is the Digital Diary. This is a small item about the size of a wallet but it can hold sixteen megabytes of information in memory. This is the same memory that the original IBM Personal Computers had, so it is a very useful item. It can easily be carried in the same folder with the breed standards. The Digital Diary contains a built-in two-hundred-year calendar as well as a telephone directory and a secret file that can hold credit card and other special information which should not be available to someone who might gain access to the computer.

LOGISTICS OF TRAVEL

Professional judges have established their travel protocols on an evolutionary basis. Most judges no longer travel by car other than to local shows, so they are frequently in contact either with the airlines directly or with travel agents. It is possible for a judge to use his own personal computer with a modem and make his own travel bookings directly through the computer. It is even possible for an individual to get travel agent discounts. The red tape involved in this type of operation forces most judges to use commercial travel agents.

Travel agents can greatly facilitate bookings when they know the travel patterns and preferences of the judge. If the judge works full-time and has departure and return time restrictions, the agent can easily work within these limitations. Most judges give a list of protocols to the agent which may include: get the cheapest possible air fare, reserve an aisle seat near the front of the plane, make sure that there is a backup flight if the original flight is canceled for some reason, or do not ever use "X" airline again.

A good travel agent can make traveling easy and save money on special air fares. The judge needs to establish whether or not he will purchase a penalty ticket. Penalty tickets range from full purchase price penalty if the flight is not used to smaller penalties of fifty percent or twenty-five percent. The larger the penalty, the lower the price of the ticket. Purchasing a ticket two or more weeks in advance also can reduce the cost. Tickets on mid-week flights are considerably more expensive than those trips that include a Saturday night. Since most dog shows are on the weekends this is usually easy to arrange. Clubs that give shows on Fridays or Mondays will frequently ask judges to stay longer or arrive earlier so as to include a Saturday night. The additional charge to the club of a night's lodging and a day's food is still cheaper than the added cost of a ticket that does not include the Saturday night. Most clubs will not honor a first class ticket charge and so state in their contract. Any judge who intends to fly first class should advise the club at the time of arranging the contract so that there can be no misunderstanding at a later date. In recent years a number of clubs ask judges to book their tickets months in advance and bill the club at that time. This does save the club on subsequent increases in plane fares. There are several clubs that have a member who is also a travel agent and they will book the tickets and mail them directly to the judge at the time of the show. This arrangement is satisfactory as long as the judge has fully explained his own time travel limitations and preferences. It is easy for a judge to have outstanding credit card bills of several thousand dollars on ticket charges at any given time. Paying these charges early to save the clubs money results in additional out-of-pocket expenses for the judge. If the clubs want tickets purchased early to save money, they should also pay for the tickets early when presented with the bill. The judge is well advised to put his plane ticket charges on his credit card for two reasons. This will usually delay the billing date until after the assignment when the judge has already been reimbursed for the cost of the ticket by the time the credit card bill arrives. This also eliminates the necessity of having to pay for a ticket that was not honored if a flight was canceled because an airline went bankrupt. A letter to the credit card company with a copy of the airline ticket is usually sufficient to have the charge removed from the bill.

Clubs normally make hotel and motel reservations for the judge well in advance of the show date. When the club sends a form to solicit the judge's preference about accommodations, there is an opportunity to indicate the number of nights required, the location of the room in the motel, and any preference for a non-smoking room. Motel accommodations range from the sub-minimal basic to the elegant, depending on the local club. Sometimes there is little choice in an area, but when there is considerable choice and the club has opted for a sub-minimal motel, judges do complain. Sometimes isolated motels do not have restaurants or the restaurants have very limited hours so the late arrivals do not have an opportunity to eat. It is wise to carry small food items just in case there is no food available at the motel. Granola-type bars can easily be packed in the luggage without adding extra weight and will carry the judge over to the next day.

The sophistication of the local clubs ranges from the almost unacceptable to the very elegant. Meal arrangements at the show may mean that the judge stands in line for a hot dog and a coke or it may mean an elegant sit-down meal with linen tablecloths and a full-course meal. The Boy Scout motto of "Be prepared" could well serve the dog show judge who must be flexible. It also helps to have a great sense of humor if he wants to keep down the level of stress that can arise on any given day.

Self-Test Questions

1. What are the limits of judging a particular breed in one area?
2. Do clubs ever extend the thirty-day, two-hundred-mile rule?
3. How long should a judge hold a date open for a club?
4. What are some methods used for keeping track of future assignments?
5. Why is it important for a judge to keep accurate records of all his assignments?
6. What kind of compensation can you expect to receive for your judging services?
7. What are some ways of making travel arrangements that work for both the judge and the club?
8. Who usually makes the hotel/motel reservations for the judge?
9. What helps a judge to keep down the level of stress that can arise on any given day?
10. Why is it important to "be prepared" regarding accommodations?

Outdoor shows are more relaxed and less formal in England. Dress is more casual and exhibitors appear to be less stressed.

sometimes required to obtain an entry visa in advance. These visas are obtained in advance from the foreign embassies here in the United States. There are maximum and minimum time periods before the trip when one may apply for the visa. These regulations change from country to country so no set of rules and regulations can be presented here. International travel is of more concern today because of the terrorist attacks on American airlines or on those airlines serving the United States.

Travel into areas known as the sources of drugs also complicates passing through customs on returning home. If, however, a judge is adventurous and very patient, overseas judging can be an exciting and worthwhile experience.

The same care must be exercised in record keeping for overseas assignments as for those in the states. Since overseas club representatives are frequently more casual about correspondence, it is at times difficult to get firm commitments about times, dates, and locations if not the assignment itself. If one is easily frustrated, it is probably best to avoid such overseas assignments.

FOREIGN KENNEL CLUBS

The following is a list of foreign kennel clubs with their addresses.

Australia Australian National Kennel Council, P.O. Box 285, Red Hill, South Victoria 3937, Australia

Austria Osterreichischer Kynologenverband, Johann Teufel-Gasse 8, A-1238 Vienna, Austria

Barbados Barbados Kennel Club, Wraysbury, Bucks, St. Thomas, Barbados, West Indies

Belgium Société Royal Saint-Hubert, Avenue de l'Armée 25, B-1040, Brussels, Belgium

Bermuda The Bermuda Kennel Club Inc., P.O. Box 1455, Hamilton 5, Bermuda HM FX

Brazil Brasil Kennel Club, Caixa Postal, 1468, Río de Janeiro, Brasil

Canada Canadian Kennel Club, 89 Skyway Ave., Suite 100, Etobicoke, Ontario M9W6R4, Canada

Caribbean The Caribbean Kennel Club, P.O. Box 737, Port of Spain, Trinidad

Chile Kennel Club de Chile, Casilla 1704, Valparaiso, Chile

Colombia Asociación Club Canino Colombiano, Calle 121 A #52-53, Bogotá, Colombia

Czech Republic Ceskomo rauska Kynologicka Onie, U Pergamenky 3, 170 00 Praha 7, Czech Republic

Denmark Dansk Kennelklub, Parkvej, DK-2680 Solrad Strand, Copenhagen, Denmark

East Africa East Africa Kennel Club, P.O. Box 14332, Westlanda, Nairobi, Kenya

England The Kennel Club, 1 Clarges St. Piccadilly, London W1Y 8AB, England

Fédération Cynologique Internationale Rue Leopold II, 14 B-6530, Thiun, Belgium

Finland Finnish Kennel Club, Kamreerintie 8, 02770, 35 P00, Finland

France Société Central Canine, 215 Rue St. Denis, 75083, Paris Cedex 02, France

Germany Verband für das Deutsche Hundewesen, West Falendamm 174, Postfach 10 41 54, D-44041 Dortmund, Germany

Greece Kennel Club of Greece, P.O. Box 5282, 146 01 N. Erythrea, Greece

Guernsey Guernsey Dog Club, Myrtle Grove, St. Jacques, Guernsey, Channel Islands

Holland Raad van Beheer op Kynologisch Gebied in Nederland, Emmalaan 16, Postbus 5901, 1007 AX Amsterdam Z., The Netherlands

Hong Kong Hong Kong Kennel Club, 3rd Floor, 28 Stanley Street, Hong Kong

Hungary Magyar Ebtenyesztok Orszagos Egyesulete, Fadrusz utca 11/a, H-1114 Budapest XL, Hungary

India South India Kennel Cub, Oakend, Ootacamund, Nilgiris 643001, India

Ireland Irish Kennel Club, 23 Earlsfort Terrace, Dublin 2, Ireland

Italy Ente Nazionale Della Cinofilia Italiana, Viale Permuda 21, 20129, Milan, Italy

Jamaica Jamaican Kennel Club, 8 Orchard Street, Kingston 5, Jamaica, West Indies

Jersey Jersey Dog Club, Clifton House, Mont Mado, St. John, Jersey, Channel Islands

Malaysia Malaysian Kennel Association, P.O. Box 559, Kuala Lampur, Malaya

Malta Malta Kennel Club, 1 Simon Flats, Dr. Zammit Street, Balzan, Malta

Mexico Federación Canofila Mexicana A.C., Malaga No. 44 Sur, 03920 México, D.F., México

Monaco Société Canine de Monaco, Palais des Congrès, Avenue d'Ostende, Monte Carlo, Monaco

Netherlands Raad Van Beheer Op Kynologisch Gebied in Nederland, Emmalaan 16-18, 1075 Amsterdam, Postbus 75901, 1070 AX, Amsterdam, The Netherlands

New Zealand New Zealand Kennel Club, Private Bag, Porirua, New Zealand

Norway Norsk Kennelklub, Nils Hansen vei 20, Box 163-Bryn, 0611, Oslo 6, Norway

Panamá Club Canino de Panamá, Apartado 6-4791, El Dorado, Panamá, Republic of Panamá

Philippines The Philippine Canine Club, RMA 206 Hillcrest Condominium, E. Rodriques Sr. Boulevard, Corner Hillcrest St., Cubao, Quezon City, Philippines

Portugal Cluba Portuguese de Canicultura, Praca D Joao da Camara, 4,3.0-Esq., Lisbon 2, Portugal

Russia Union of Canine Organizations of Russia, E. Yersusalimsky, Mockaba, O OB HCKOE W 1-A, Moscow, Russia

Scotland The Scottish Kennel Club, 3 Brunswick Place, Edinburgh EH7 5 HP, Scotland

Singapore The Singapore Kennel Club, 275f Selegie Complex, Selegie Road, Singapore 7

Slovenia Kinoloska Zveza Slovenije, Ilirska 27, 6100 Ljubijana, Slovenia

South Africa Kennel Union of Southern Africa, 6th Floor, Bree Castle, 68 Bree St., Cape Town 8001, South Africa

Spain Real Sociedad Central de Fomento de las Razas en España, Los Madrazos 20, Madrid, Spain

Sri Lanka The Kennel Association of Sri Lanka, 19 Race Course Avenue, Colombo 7, Sri Lanka

Sweden Svenska Kennelklubben, Rinkebysvangen 70, S-163 85 Spanga, Sweden

Switzerland Stammbuchsekretariat der Schweizerische Kynologische Gesellschaft, Wildparkstrasse 253, 4656 Wil bei Olten, Switzerland

United States American Kennel Club, 260 Madison Avenue, New York, New York 10010

Uruguay Kennel Club Uruguayo, Avenida Uruguay 864, Montevideo, Uruguay

Venezuela Federación Canina Venezuela, Apartado 88665, Caracas 1080-A, Venezuela

Wales Welsh Kennel Club, Plasnewydd, Broadway, Builth Wells, Powys 4D2 3DB, Wales

The largest international kennel club organization is the Fédération Cynologique Internationale which has its headquarters in Belgium. This is the controlling parent organization for kennel club activity in the following countries: Argentina, Austria, Belgium, Brazil, Czech Republic, Denmark, Finland, France, Germany, Greece, Hungary, Holland, Italy, Luxembourg, Mexico, Monaco, Morocco, Norway, Poland, Portugal, Spain, Sweden, Switzerland, and Yugoslavia.

The Fédération Cynologique Internationale, or simply the FCI, was founded in 1911 with only four member countries: Austria, Belgium, Germany, and Holland. It has since expanded to include sixty-five different countries and recognizes 335 individual breeds. This organization maintains stud books, controls breed standards, and regulates discipline and international judging standards. In addition, the FCI recognizes the Certificate of Aptitude, Championship International, Beauty (CACIB) and the Certificate of Aptitude, Championship International, Trials (CACIT). These two certificates are awarded at international shows only. The Certificate of Aptitude, Championship (CAC) is awarded at national shows.

Self-Test Questions

1. Are international breed standards different from the standards of the AKC?
2. What are some special problems of international judging?
3. What are some special considerations regarding international airline travel?
4. Why should you pay extra attention to your record keeping for overseas assignments?
5. What is the largest international kennel club organization?
6. Where is this organization located?
7. For what countries is it the controlling parent organization for kennel club activity?
8. What are some of the activities of the Fédération Cynologique Internationale?
9. What certificates are awarded by the FCI?

Appendix: A Comparative Study of Similar Breeds

Difficulty in judging certain breeds arises from time to time when these breeds are similar to each other. A number of breeds that have a common historical development also have a common anatomical development. Undertaking a comparative study of two or more breeds is an excellent way to develop a thorough understanding of both the development of the breed as well as its present-day status. The following study could serve as such an analysis and provide a pattern for similar studies in other breeds.

HISTORY OF ORIENTAL BREEDS

There are a number of breeds that originated in the Orient that today have similar characteristics. While there is a degree of similarity between these breeds, there is also a good deal of difference in size, structure, and in quantity of coat and coat pattern. It is possible to hypothesize that all these breeds came from common ancestors and that the differences that exist today are the results of breedings that took place through the years when little or no thought was given to maintaining consistency of type.

The Oriental breeds of this study have the foreshortened face and the tail, which is usually curled, carried up and over the back. These breeds include the Lhasa Apso, the Tibetan Spaniel, the Tibetan Terrier, the Pekingese, and the Shih Tzu.

There seems to be a close relationship in conformation between the Lhasa Apso, the Shih Tzu, the Tibetan Spaniel, and the Tibetan Terrier. The Lhasa Apso and the Shih Tzu are quite similar and were undoubtedly even more so a century or two ago. The Pekingese is similar to these two breeds in certain respects, differing mainly in coat, head piece, and gait. The Tibetan Spaniel differs from the Lhasa Apso in head and coat. The Tibetan Terrier has certain characteristics similar to those of the Tibetan Spaniel but is larger and has a more Terrier-type head.

LHASA APSO

The Lhasa Apso dates back a thousand years or more in Tibet, the country of its origin. While recorded history of the Lhasa Apso is most difficult to verify, there are strong indications that the breed is among the oldest in the world.

Because of the almost complete isolation of Tibet, little was known about it by the outside world. The Lhasa Apso, moreover, belonged only to the Dalai Lama or to the rulers of other monasteries. They were kept hidden and well protected from strangers and were seen only by those who had the privilege of entering the monasteries and the sacred villages. Early travelers, not enjoying this special privilege, were, therefore, completely unaware of the existence of the little sacred dogs.

While certain qualities of conformation such as color were regarded as important, the Lhasa Apso was really considered an obedience type of dog since his role and training were intended to serve a special function in the palace. This lack of special interest in conformation resulted in a great variety of sizes. The lack of uniformity in the breeding program genetically locked certain variables into the breed, which helps to explain the "throwbacks" that appear even today in carefully controlled breeding programs of professional Lhasa Apso breeders.

Among the characteristics the Lhasa Apso shares with the other breeds of Tibetan origin are the dense coat and the curly tail carried up and over the back. Dogs living in a cold climate and at a high altitude developed dense coats through the process of natural evolution. Other Tibetan breeds of dogs share the same coat and tail characteristics.

The Tibetan Spaniel was considered primarily a beautiful lap dog, admired for its looks rather than for any function it might serve. The Tibetan Terrier was the more common breed, for it was raised in many parts of Tibet. It is the true Terrier representative, both in disposition and conformation.

TIBETAN SPANIEL

A number of things that have been said about the history of the Lhasa Apso can also be said about the Tibetan Spaniel. It has the same country of origin, the same casual breeding program, and centuries of isolation from outside influences.

A major influence in the development of the Tibetan Spaniel was the Buddhist religion. Buddha was born in 557 B.C. and with him was established the cult of the lion. The lion was the animal symbol of Buddha, for he was able to change himself into a lion during moments of danger and defend himself with the courage of a lion. Since lions were not native to Tibet, an animal substitute had to be found and this turned out to be the small, lion-like dogs. These dogs were golden in color and carried a mane-like ruff around the neck and over the shoulders.

TIBETAN TERRIER

The same set of geographical and historical circumstances that influenced the development of the Lhasa Apso and the Tibetan Spaniel hold true for the Tibetan Terrier.

Authorities believe that the breed may be as much as two thousand years old. Like the other two Tibetan breeds, the Tibetan Terrier was a dog of the monasteries but was also found in the homes of the nobles. However, during the seventeenth century there were riots in the capital of Lhasa and in order to protect these dogs, some of them were sent to isolated monasteries in the interior of the country. The breeding of these dogs, therefore, followed a slightly different pattern. One of the valleys where some of these dogs were raised was nearly destroyed by an earthquake. Dogs that survived from this Lost Valley of Tibet were considered to possess a special charm of good luck.

The Tibetan Terrier was never sold but was occasionally offered as a special gift to a departing visiting dignitary. During periods of great instability when Tibet was invaded by hordes from the West, dogs were carried off as part of the spoils of war. It is believed that the Tibetan Terrier was carried back to Europe. He is thought to be one of the ancestors of the Hungarian Puli. The Tibetan Terrier was never a working dog in its native land. There he was never anything more than a companion dog or an object of worship.

PEKINGESE

The Pekingese is known to have existed for hundreds of years. There is concrete evidence of the early existence of the breed both in literature and in art.

Small lap dogs or ladies' dogs existed in many parts of the world centuries before the birth of Christ. These little dogs were popular both in China and in Japan in the East and in Egypt and in the West. They were carefully protected and highly valued by their owners, who were always members of the ruling class.

The title "Lion Dog" was used to refer to a number of small Oriental dogs in addition to the Pekingese. Among them are the Lhasa Apso, the Maltese, and the Shih Tzu. It was not until recent years that the specific names for the various breeds were regularized. The Pekingese was frequently referred to as the Pekingese Spaniel or the Pekingese Pug even at the beginning of this century.

When the breed began to be exported in larger numbers the name was shortened.

Interest was generated in using the small palace dogs as a symbolic representation of the lion, which was already a symbol itself. The small royal dogs that existed at the time were the Lo-Sze, which was the ancestor of the Pug, the Peiching Kou or Peking Dog, and a small Maltese-like dog. Undoubtedly these dogs were crossbred to produce the most lion-like dog possible. The breeding of the dogs was the responsibility of the eunuchs who were part of the royal household. Competition to breed the best specimens would have been keenest if a eunuch wished to gain royal favor.

The body coat of early dogs was probably shaved to give an illusion of a huge lion-like ruff or mane, but selective breedings subsequently could have eliminated the necessity of this particular grooming technique. There is even some evidence that on occasions the nose of the Pekingese was shortened surgically to make him more ferocious looking and to give greater contrast to the mane.

SHIH TZU

It appears that the Shih Tzu had two separate origins and that it was not, in fact, until into the twentieth century that the one type dominated over the other.

The Pekingese and the Lhasa Apso were exchanged as gifts between the royal families of China and Tibet. The differences in size and type led their owners to do some experimental breeding to see what a cross between the two breeds might produce. Those dogs produced in China were smaller because repeated crosses were made back to the smaller Pekingese. In Tibet the crosses were somewhat larger because they were taken back to the larger Lhasa Apso.

Since dog breeding in the royal palace in China was the responsibility of the eunuchs, the situation was more regulated than it was in Tibet. As a result the dogs produced from this cross-breeding program were more controlled. The eunuchs took pride in their work and were conscientious in their efforts to create a new breed.

Shih Tzu-type dogs from Tibet came out through India where they were discovered by the British. Shih Tzu-type dogs from China were available to the British through Peking, Shanghai, and Hong Kong. Because of their size and consistency of type, the dogs from China were selected over those from Tibet.

ANATOMY

The function for which a dog was created or bred was the major determining factor in the anatomy of the dog. Guard dogs were bred to be large and well-muscled. Herding dogs were short-coupled for ease of movement and the ability to change directions rapidly. Sight Hounds were higher stationed for movement over open land while Terriers were shorter legged so they could go to ground. Toy or companion dogs had no particular anatomical requirements so they could come in different sizes and shapes.

The Oriental dogs represented in this study were strictly companion dogs and as such physical needs were not of major importance. This is evidenced by the slow labored gait of the Pekingese. The only requirement for some of these dogs was to bark to warn their master of the arrival of a stranger. Personality was the most important quality of these companion dogs.

LHASA APSO

Of the five Oriental breeds represented here, the Lhasa Apso is a medium-sized dog. Ideally he is about ten to eleven inches tall at the withers. Weight would be in proportion to his height and would be in the range of eighteen to twenty-two pounds. Larger specimens are seen in the ring today but they tend to be on the coarse side and lose the characteristics that are typical of the breed.

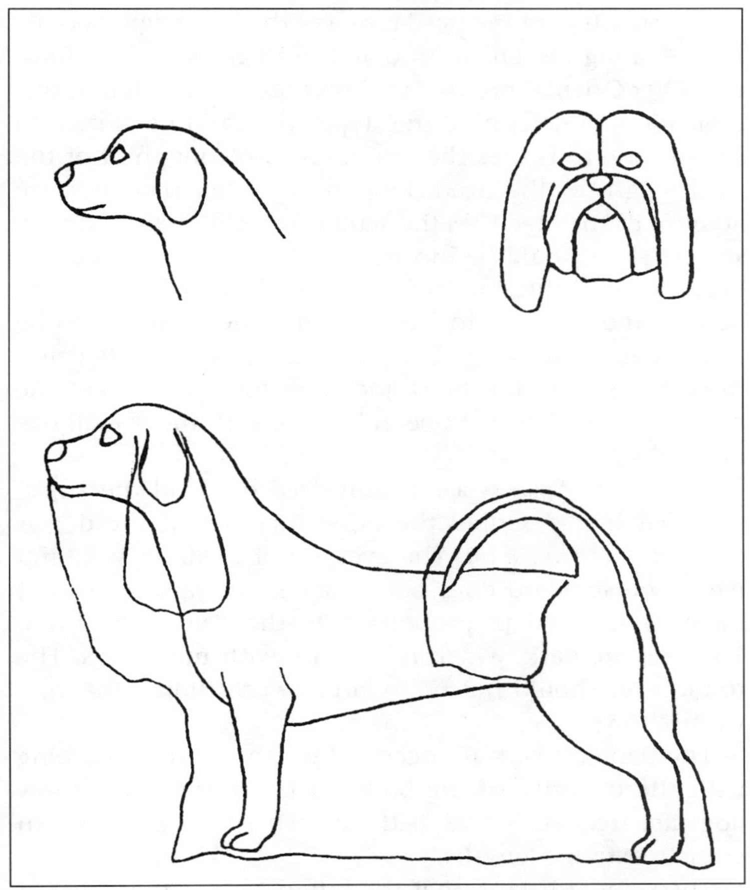

Lhasa Apso: Head study and side profile.

The general appearance is that of a heavily coated dog with a flowing coat that reaches the floor. In recent years this is the rule and it is difficult for a shorter coated dog to win. Twenty-five years ago the length of coat was several inches above the floor, but tastes and grooming techniques have changed and competition now demands that the full flowing coat be the standard.

The structure of the head is one of the key judging points in evaluating the Lhasa Apso and distinguishing him from the other Oriental breeds. Head proportions are vital in this evaluation to determine true type. The ratio of muzzle to skull is one to two as the muzzle is to be one-third of the total length of the head. Proportions other than this are atypical of the breed. As the skull is to be narrow, a square-shaped skull would be incorrect and would have incorrect balance. Until the standard was revised, the muzzle was to be one and one-half inches long and the skull was to be only three inches long. These precise measurements determine the size of the head and, therefore, the size of the body if the head were to be in balance with the overall size of the dog.

The Lhasa Apso is a medium-sized dog and the adjective that best describes the other qualities of the dog is also the word *medium*. The eyes are of medium size, and while the standard does not so state, the ears are also of medium size and in proportion to the size of the head. The eyes are dark, which is the case with most dogs. The round eyes should not be so large or protruding that any white shows.

The pendant ears are heavily furnished and in keeping with the quantity of the body coat. Ear fringes of show dogs are frequently wrapped between shows so they can grow to extreme length.

The standard states that the bite is to be either level or slightly undershot. If the incisors are to be in a broad, straight line, it is almost impossible for the bite to be level. One fault that is becoming more frequent in the ring in the United States is the scissors bite. This changes the shape of the muzzle, for it narrows it considerably as the scissors bite requires that the incisors be in a curved line rather than in a straight line. American breeders have not yet faced the reality and the consequences of the problem they are creating.

The body of the Lhasa Apso is longer from the point of shoulder to the buttocks than it is tall at the withers. Dogs that are longer than they are tall tend to move with more freedom. The dog has good rib spring and the rear is slightly more narrow than the front. It is not as pear-shaped as the Pekingese, but there is enough difference that it does have consequences for the gait.

While the forelegs are to be straight, a great number of exhibits in the ring today have curved front legs. Some are so exaggerated that they have what might be called a Pekingese front. This is usually the result of an overly expanded rib cage tending toward the barrel-shape. The coat covers this condition so ringside spectators cannot appreciate the problem.

Hindquarters are to have good angulation. Many dogs today have bones in the hind legs that are too long for the dog and are out of balance with his overall size. This causes the dog to stand too tall in the rear. To mask this condition the handler will pull the hocks back when posing the dog to lower the rear and make the topline level. This over-angulates the rear. This can easily be checked by feeling the front of the hocks to determine whether or not they are directly below a line extended down from the rear of the buttocks. The greater the distance between these two lines, the greater is the fault.

The movement of the dog is described as free and jaunty. This description does not really define the unique quality of the movement of the Lhasa Apso. Since the dog is somewhat narrower in the rear than in the front, he has a tendency to have a slight roll. This was the standard gait of Lhasa Apsos in the past. As dogs become higher stationed and more rangy, the difference in width between the front and rear quarters is disappearing and the dog is losing his typical movement.

The coat of the average show specimen today reaches to the floor. Many exhibitors equate quantity with quality and are ignoring the importance of coat texture. Most of the overly abundant coats are of incorrect texture as they are entirely too soft. It is easy to stand ringside and evaluate texture by the quantity of coat and the way it flows or does not flow when the dog gaits. The correct coat is slightly on the harsh side which, along with the undercoat, gives the dog the good protection that he would need to survive the temperatures at thirteen thousand feet. Many dogs with the incorrect, excessive coats are also barrel-ribbed, which makes the dog look out of balance as being too wide for his length.

Colors are no longer rated with a preference although in the past, in keeping with the lion tradition, the golden dog was preferred over any other color. Blacks and particolored dogs had a hard time winning in the ring under these circumstances. The American Kennel Club standard lists only one serious fault and that is low tail carriage.

TIBETAN SPANIEL

While the height of the Tibetan Spaniel is the same as that of the Lhasa Apso, there are great differences between the two breeds. The weight limitations for the Tibetan Spaniel are between nine and fifteen pounds, some seven to nine pounds lighter than the Lhasa Apso. This clearly indicates that there will be considerable difference in the size and shape of the body of the dog. Both dogs are described as longer from point of shoulder to buttocks than the dog is tall at the withers.

The skull is domed and is somewhat larger in proportion to the muzzle than it is in some other breeds. This creates a more refined muzzle than might be expected in a dog of this size. While the standard does not so state, the proportion of the muzzle to skull is about one to three. This is different than the ratio in the Lhasa Apso and is one of the distinguishing breed differences. The standard calls for the slightly undershot mouth but also accepts a level bite provided that there is sufficient width between the canines.

The dark oval eyes are set well apart and are of medium size. Because of the somewhat higher set of the ears and the feathering they carry, the eyes at first appear to be small by comparison. However, by encircling the head with the hands and eliminating the illusion of extra width that the ears give, it is easy to see that the eyes are truly medium in size in proportion to the skull alone.

The ears are set on higher than any of the other Oriental breeds and are frequently lifted when the dog is excited, making them appear even more high-set. They frame the skull rather than blend in with the overall outline of the head. This is distinctive of the breed.

The neck is short and appears even more so in dogs that carry an abundant mane or shawl around the shoulders. The more abundant the mane, the shorter the neck seems. Hand-checking is important to determine if the neck is too short or merely gives the illusion that it is.

The body of the Tibetan Spaniel has neither the breadth nor the depth of the Lhasa Apso. This explains the great difference in the weight descriptions for the two breeds. The size and proportion of the body is in keeping with a higher stationed, more elegant dog. The dog does have good spring of ribs which is in keeping with his overall size. Front and rear quarters are approximately the same width so the Tibetan Spaniel does not have the rolling gait of the Lhasa Apso.

The shoulders are well laid back but the forelegs are slightly bowed. This does not interfere with the movement of the dog as the bow is so slight. The hocks are short and parallel which produces good strong rear movement. Stifles are only moderately bent.

The foot of the Tibetan Spaniel distinguishes it from the other Tibetan breeds. It is the only standard to call for the hare foot. The round foot of the other breeds is considered

Tibetan Spaniel: Head study and side profile.

a fault for this dog. The feathering on the feet and between the toes is usually left untrimmed, which makes the feet appear even larger than they are.

The tail set is high, which is typical of these breeds, and is carried over the back. Should the tail drop when the dog is standing the dog is not to be penalized. The tail is heavily plumed, which is typical of these breeds.

The Tibetan Spaniel has the typical double coat. The fact that the coat is silky distinguishes it from the coat of other breeds. It is finer and, therefore, lies closer to the body. It does not add the appearance of bulk to the frame. The ears are well furnished and the hair is longer on the tail and on the the buttocks. Bitches are forgiven for having a less abundant coat than the males. There is no color preference for coat and no individual colors are even listed.

The American Kennel Club lists a series of faults under each section of the standard. This situation tends to lead the judge to fault judge if he is not careful.

TIBETAN TERRIER

The ideal Tibetan Terrier should stand between 15 inches and 16 inches. This means that he is considerably taller than the Lhasa Apso. There is an acceptable range of between 14 inches and 17 inches. In addition, the dog is square from point of shoulder to buttocks, rather than longer as in the Lhasa Apso and the Tibetan Spaniel.

Considering the history of the Tibetan Terrier, it is not surprising that he is a bigger dog. He was not confined to the monasteries nor to private homes as were the other two Tibetan breeds and, therefore, he had more opportunity for outside exercise and size limitations were not that important. Instead of breeding for medium to small size, the limits were allowed to be more flexible.

The standard says that the Tibetan Terrier is a medium-sized dog, and he is in comparison to dogs in general, but in comparison to the other four breeds in this study he is tall. The fact that he is square creates the impression that he is even taller than he really is. This illusion can be checked during judging by using the span of the hand to verify the correct balance.

The ratio of the skull to the muzzle is one of the key characteristics in identifying the correct head type in the Tibetan Terrier. The ratio is one to one, meaning that the muzzle and the skull are of equal length. There are specimens seen in the ring today that have incorrect muzzle-to-skull ratios. Some of these dogs are winning and being included in breeding programs, which will only create more problems.

The stop is not as great as it is in either the Lhasa Apso or in the Tibetan Spaniel. The longer muzzle explains this difference. The skull is proportionately more narrow than the other two Tibetan breeds. The skull is only moderately curved.

The eyes are large, dark, and more intent. They are set fairly wide apart. The V-shaped ears are pendant and well furnished. If the ear fringes are wrapped they can reach great length. Longer and longer ear fringes are appearing in the ring today and do impress many people, so it can only be assumed that this trend will continue on for some time.

The standard accepts the scissors bite, the reverse scissors bite, the level bite, and a slightly undershot bite. The standard for the mouth is really responsible for a serious problem in the breed. A scissors bite requires more curve to jaw for the incisor teeth while the level and reverse scissors do not. As the jaw takes on more of a curve the muzzle narrows and changes the balance of the head. The level bite and the undershot bite would underscore the breed's Oriental heritage.

The standard calls for a level back when the dog is in motion. Since the croup is level, the tail would be set on high. It is carried up and over the back as it is in the other four breeds.

The shoulders are well laid back and the forelegs are straight and parallel. The hind legs are well bent at the stifle and the hocks are short. The feet are round and have no arch, which means that they are really flat like the Pekingese. If the forequarters and the hindquarters are as

Tibetan Terrier: Head study and side profile.

they should be, the dog is balanced and should move straight and true.

The Tibetan Terrier is to move in a straight line with the hind legs tracking on the path of the forelegs. If the dog is correctly balanced this is what will happen. However, since the dog is squarely built he must be balanced front and rear or he will not be able to move the way he should. If he is unbalanced he will sidewind or take some other diversionary action to avoid stepping on his own front feet.

The coat in texture is between the firm coat of the Lhasa Apso and the silky coat of the Tibetan Spaniel. It is a double coat and carries a reasonable quantity of woolly undercoat. The standard accepts all colors without exception. It also states that the coat should not reach the ground so that a rectangle of light can be seen under the dog.

PEKINGESE

The outstanding characteristic of the Pekingese is his lion-like appearance. This is mainly achieved by the coat that he carries and by the mane-like ruff around his shoulders. While the lion color was originally the most sought-after coat color, other colors are seen in the ring today.

The head is the key to the Pekingese type. The standard assigns forty percent of its scale of points to the head. The correct head, viewed from the front, is rectangular in shape and is wider than it is high. In keeping with the rectangular shape, the skull is flat. The large, round eyes are set wide apart adding to the illusion of the skull width.

The stop is exaggerated in that the nose is almost recessed. A line drawn from the lower jaw to the top of the skull will just touch the tip of the nose. Only in the Bulldog does this same condition exist. The Bulldog standard allocates thirty-nine points out of one hundred to the head.

The muzzle is very short, but it is broad. The standard only says that the mouth is not to be overshot and that the teeth must not show. Most exhibitors do not want the judge to examine the bite as they say that it upsets the dog. The judge must check, however, if only to determine that the dog does indeed have teeth.

The ears are set level with the skull and the ear leathers are to be relatively short as they must not reach below the muzzle. The long ear feathering creates the illusion that the ears are quite long. The ears are described as heart-shaped.

The dog is slightly longer than he is tall. The body of the Pekingese is somewhat unusual in that it is pear-shaped. The chest is broad and capacious and narrows to a distinct waist. The hindquarters are markedly more narrow than the chest. This difference in width between the forequarters and the hindquarters of the dog gives him his unique rolling gait.

The forelegs are heavily boned and short, which means that there is little space between the keel and the ground. Since the body of the Pekingese is almost suspended between the forelegs rather than resting on top of them, the forelegs must curve slightly inward below the elbows to give the dog stability. This is what is commonly referred to as the Pekingese front. This characteristic can become overly exaggerated and would, therefore, not be typical of the breed.

The hind legs have more refined bone than the forelegs. Because of the narrowness of the hips the hind legs are set closer together than are the forelegs. While the hind legs are parallel, when viewed from the rear they are not perpendicular to the ground. The hocks tend to slope slightly. The feet are described as flat and not round. The standard allows both front and rear feet to turn out.

As with the other Oriental breeds, the tail of the Pekingese is well feathered and carried up and over the back. It may be straight or hang slightly to either side.

While the American Kennel Club standard assigns only fifteen points to the coat, most exhibitors feel that the coat is the breed's crowning glory and is worth considerably more than the fifteen points allocated to it.

The Pekingese is a double-coated breed. The undercoat is thick, which gives bulk to the outer coat and makes the

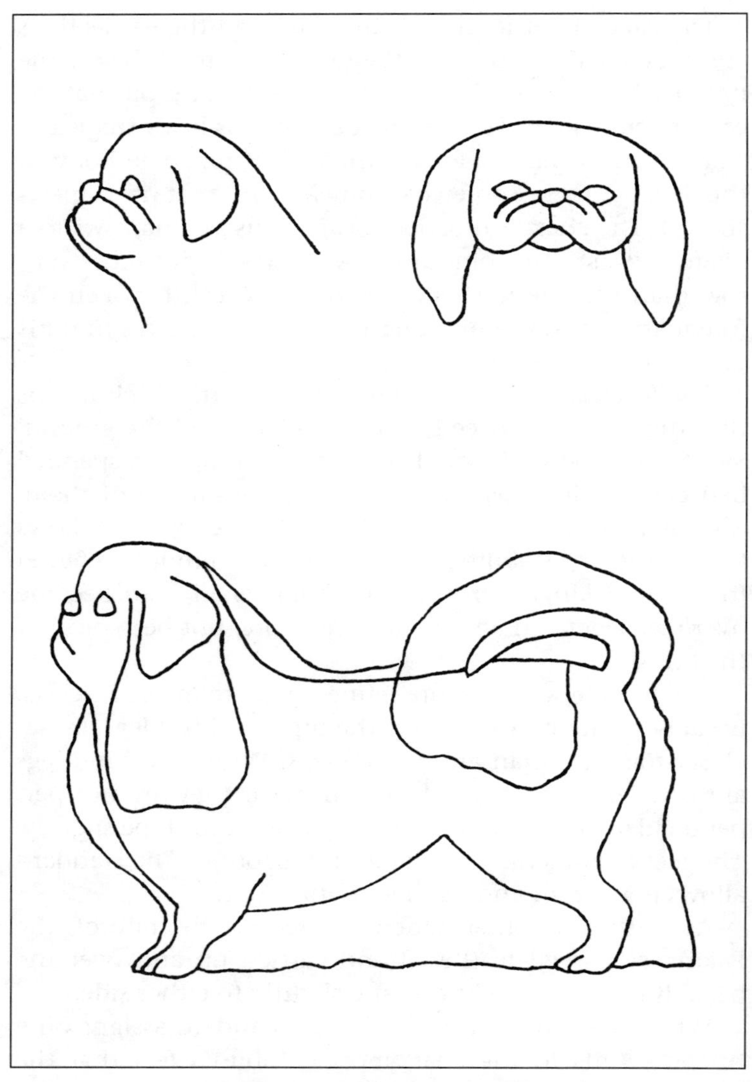

Pekingese: Head study and side profile.

breed look more massive than it really is. The top coat is coarse by contrast and with good grooming techniques can reach great length. One fad seen recently in the United States is to wrap the hair on the rear of the dog so that it reaches great length, which will serve as a train when the dog is gaiting in the ring. This adds nothing to the dog and destroys the profile balance which is important in this breed.

The American Kennel Club standard accepts all colors including parti-color dogs. The parti color is to be evenly broken.

SHIH TZU

It is interesting to note that the Shih Tzu is placed in the Utility Group in England, but is in the Toy Group in the Unites States. It was probably the weight that classified it as a Toy here in the States, but some suspect it was also an effort to avoid confusion with the Lhasa Apso, since many people do not understand the differences between the two breeds.

The Shih Tzu is a heavily coated Oriental dog that is markedly longer than it is tall. He has a jaunty, happy gait and an outgoing and friendly personality.

The head is round and broad and in balance to the size of the dog. Since there is considerable variance in the size of different specimens of the breed, this balance is of extreme importance. A number of dogs are being exhibited today that have heads that are too small and out of proportion to the body.

The eyes are large, dark, and round but are not to be prominent. They are set wide apart which gives the dog his distinct expression. The eyes of dogs carrying liver pigmentation will be lighter. Eyes that are too prominent will show white which will destroy the expression.

The ears are set on below the top of the skull and the leathers are on the large size. The ears are heavily feathered and when wrapped will reach great lengths.

Shih Tzu: Head study and side profile.

The muzzle, which is to be no longer than one inch, is square. The nose is set no lower than the bottom of the eyes and may rise even above this imaginary line. The standard states that the overshot mouth is a fault.

The topline of the dog, between the withers and the root of the tail, is longer than the dog is tall. When considering the additional distance between the withers and the point of shoulders, the dog does appear long when seen in profile. Since the dog is described as short- coupled, the extra length comes from the length of back rather than from the loin area.

With the influence of the Pekingese in the creation of the breed, it is understandable that straightness of bone might be a problem for the breed.

The hindquarters do not have the contrast that is found in the Pekingese. The hind legs are not close set but are in line with the forequarters. This can only mean that the forequarters and the hindquarters are of the same width. The hocks are short and the feet rounded.

The tail is set on high and carried up and over the back. The curve of the tail is such that it is approximately the same height above the top line as is the head.

The Shih Tzu has a double coat. The undercoat is dense and the top coat is more silky than it is coarse. The texture of coat is different than that of the Pekingese. All colors are permissible including the parti-colored dogs.

The standard lists the ideal height as being between nine and ten and one-half inches with absolute limits being between eight and eleven inches. The range for weight is between nine and sixteen pounds, which is close to the nine to fifteen pounds of the Tibetan Spaniel.

The 1989 revision of the standard made a change in the section on gait. This change is having considerable effect in the show ring today. It states that the dog must not be raced nor strung-up with the lead. Showing a dog on a loose lead has affected placements in the ring. Dogs with bad shoulders, short necks, and weak rears are now evident for all ringside spectators to see. It has caused much unhappiness among breeders who have these traits locked into their breeding program.

KEY DIFFERENCES BETWEEN THE BREEDS

While the five Oriental breeds undoubtedly share a common heritage and still today have many characteristics that are the same, there are still certain differences between the breeds that are the keys to breed type.

In evaluating any breed the judge should have a priority list of those elements that are most important in his evaluation of an individual exhibit. A common priority list might be arranged in the following order:

1. Type
2. Balance
3. Soundness
4. Condition
5. Showmanship

Type has to be the single most important element in judging any breed, for it is precisely this quality that distinguishes one breed from another. A dog may be balanced, sound, and in good condition, but if he does not look like the breed he has little or no merit and would certainly not be included in a breeding program.

The areas for distinguishing breed type in these five Oriental breeds are as follows: head, forequarters, body, hindquarters, coat, and gait.

HEADS

The charts that follow show the heads of the five breeds to explain the difference in head type.

The heads in profile are arranged in descending order starting with the Tibetan Terrier, which has the longest muzzle, to the Pekingese, which has the shortest muzzle.

The Tibetan Terrier has a muzzle that has a one-to-one ratio with the skull. This means that the skull is equal in length to the muzzle.

The Lhasa Apso has a one-to-two ratio between the muzzle and the skull so that the muzzle is only one-third the total length of the head. The standard used to have a one and one-half inch muzzle length measurement in it, but several years ago the parent club dropped the precise measurement. The reason for this is that the breed was getting larger and larger and the size limitation either had to be ignored or the dog's head would be grossly out of proportion with the body. This, unfortunately, has led to ever larger dogs in the ring. Dogs of twenty-five to twenty-eight pounds can be seen in the ring today.

The muzzle of the Tibetan Spaniel is approximately one-fourth of the length of the head, thus having a one-to-three ratio with the skull.

The Shih Tzu muzzle is one-fifth of the length of the head as it has a one-to-four ratio with the skull. In some instances this ratio is even one to six, which is even more reminiscent of the Pekingese heritage.

These ratios are important in determining true breed type. When the ratios are out of balance the dog does not have a typical expression and is, therefore, not a good representative of the breed.

The right column of the chart is presented to show another distinguishing characteristic of these Oriental breeds. This element has to do with the angle of the muzzle in relationship with the skull and the stop and the effect it has on the expression of the dog.

The heads are arranged in the same order with the Tibetan Terrier at the top and the Pekingese at the bottom. A line has been drawn across the muzzle in order to show the placement of the nose in relationship to the eye.

When looking directly into the face of the Tibetan Terrier, it is noted that the nose is slightly below the bottom of the eye. This gives a slightly down-faced expression to the breed. The length of muzzle is the key factor here, but in dogs that have the very short muzzle this is not the case.

Comparative Head Studies

(Opposite page)

This study shows the relationship between the length of muzzle and the position of the nose. The line drawn across the bridge of the nose passes below the eye of the Tibetan Terrier. On the Lhasa Apso the line is even with the lower eyelid. In the Tibetan Spaniel the line is just above the upper edge of the lower eyelid. In the Shih Tzu the line is higher up the eyeball. In the Pekingese the line can cross through the upper half of the eyeball.

Left column:
Comparative head study in profile.

1. *Tibetan Terrier—length ratio of 1 muzzle to 1 skull.*
2. *Lhasa Apso—ratio of 1 muzzle to 2 skull.*
3. *Tibetan Spaniel—ratio 1 muzzle to 3 skull.*
4. *Shih Tzu—ratio 1 muzzle to 4 skull.*
5. *Pekingese—does not have a ratio as the nose is recessed below a straight line drawn from the chin to the forehead.*

Right column:
Comparative head study in front view.

1. *Tibetan Terrier.*
2. *Lhasa Apso.*
3. *Tibetan Spaniel.*
4. *Shih Tzu.*
5. *Pekingese.*

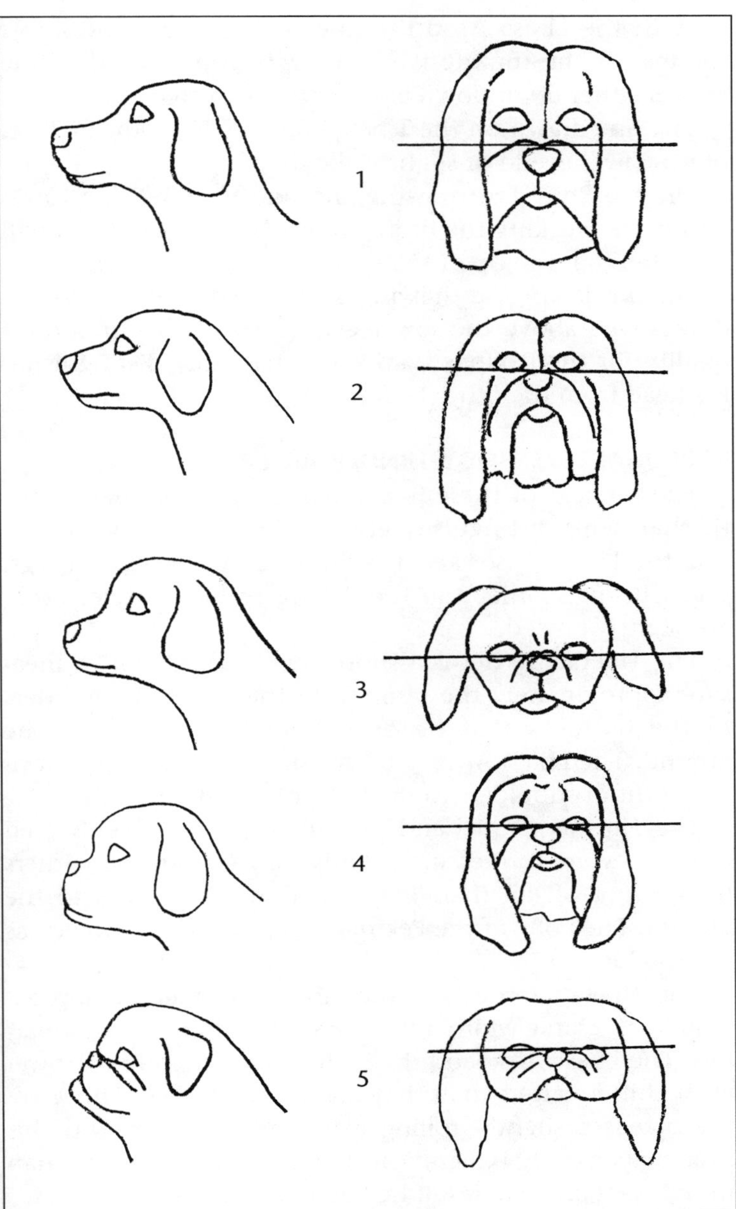
1
2
3
4
5

With the Lhasa Apso the line is just at the bottom of the eye. If the muzzle is too long or too short this line moves either up or down and alters the expression.

The line drawn on the Tibetan Spaniel is about the level of the lower eyelid or slightly above it.

On the Shih Tzu drawing the line is above the lower eyelid. In checking the profile of the Shih Tzu head, it will be noted that the tip of the nose of is slightly raised.

On the Pekingese drawing it is noted that the line is drawn well above the lower eyelid. This is an important quality for the Pekingese and one that truly distinguishes his head from the other heads.

FOREQUARTERS, BODY, HINDQUARTERS

The forelegs of these five breeds is another characteristic that helps distinguish between them. The Tibetan Terrier, the Lhasa Apso, and the Shih Tzu have straight legs. The Tibetan Spaniel and the Pekingese have forelegs that are slightly bowed.

The Tibetan Terrier is a short dog, in that he is to measure approximately the same from the point of shoulders to the buttocks that he does from the withers to the ground. The Lhasa Apso is to measure slightly longer from the point of shoulders to the buttocks than he is tall.

The Tibetan Spaniel and the Shih Tzu are longer-bodied dogs. They are to measure slightly longer from the withers to the root of tail than they do from the withers to the ground. The body of the Pekingese is described, however, as not too long.

The Tibetan Terrier and the Tibetan Spaniel are approximately the same width at the rib cage and at the hindquarters. The Lhasa Apso and the Shih Tzu are slightly narrower at the hindquarters than they are at the rib cage. This gives the breeds a slightly rolling gait. The Pekingese with his pear-shaped body is significantly narrower in the rear than in the front and as a result he has a decided roll to his gait.

COAT

Coat is another element that distinguishes the breeds from each other. The coat of the Tibetan Terrier is described as fine and it is somewhat softer that the hard coat of the Lhasa Apso. The Tibetan Spaniel has a silky coat and the Shih Tzu has a coat that tends toward the silky side although it is not as fine as that of the Tibetan Spaniel. The coat of the Pekingese is coarse. This, along with the dense undercoat, is what gives the Pekingese a coat that will stand out from the body and form the ruff or mane.

FAULTS

Under the American Kennel Club standard, specific individual faults are listed. In the latest revision of the standard the American Shih Tzu Club has included a general statement about faults, but then goes ahead and lists individual faults as well.

The major faults with these Oriental breeds would be those which would cause the dog to lose the particular qualities which would destroy the evidence of his Oriental heritage. These would include the head piece, the coat, and the distinctive gaits of the breeds.

CONCLUSION

While the judging of Oriental breeds is really no different from judging of any other breed, the importance of the hands-on examination must be stressed. This is truly the only way to see through the coat and find the real essence of the breed.

There are general similarities between the five breeds included in this study, but there are also distinguishing differences and these must be properly evaluated if the judging is to be conscientious and correct. Learning the subtleties of these breeds and being able to apply this knowledge is rightly expected of the judge. The exhibitor pays the entry fee and, therefore, merits a professional and impartial opinion based on training and experience.

Glossary

abdomen—the belly, the area between the end of the rib cage and the hindquarters.

Achilles tendon—the long, strong muscle that connects the hock to the lower thigh.

action—a general term used frequently to describe gait or movement.

almond eye—term used to describe the shape of the eye resembling the shape of an almond nut.

amble—a gait in which both legs on one side move almost together. The rear foot lifts from the ground barely before the front foot. It is a slower gait than the pace.

anatomy—the term used to describe the structure of the dog and includes the skeletal and muscle system.

angulation—describes the angles between adjoining bones as in the angle between the scapula and the humerus or between the pelvis and the femur.

ankle—the hock joint in the dog.

ankylosis—a fusion of bones that is not normal, as in the tail.

apex—the occiput or the rear of the skull.

apple head—describes the rounded skull as in the Chihuahua.

apron—longer hair on the lower neck and chest.

aquiline—describes the rounding or curve on the top of the muzzle where it dips to the nose.

arch—the gentle rise as the arch over the loin or on the nape of the neck.

arched toes—synonymous with cat foot.

arm—the front leg of the dog. The upper arm is the humerus and the lower arm is the radius-ulna.

articulation—the joint that is formed between two bones that are moveable.

back—that area of the topline between the withers and the loin.
back skull—the part of the skull behind the eyes.
badger—a color which includes a mixture of hair that is white, black, brown, and gray.
balance—a general term used to describe the relationship and ratio of the various parts of the dog.
bandy—term used to describe legs that are bowed.
barrel chest—describes a rib cage that is round rather than oval.
barrel hocks—hocks that are bowed out, synonymous with bow hocks.
barrel ribs—ribs rounded like barrel staves.
bat ears—erect ears that are stiff and curve slightly forward as in the French Bulldog.
beady eyes—small eyes.
beard—hair on the chin, usually a mixture of soft and harsh hair.
beefy—a dog that is excessively muscled.
belton—a ticking pattern of coat color as in the English Setter.
bitch—a female dog.
bite—describes how the upper and lower teeth meet, i.e. level, even, scissors, overshot, or undershot.
blade—shoulder blade or scapula.
blanket—an area of color over the back and sides of a dog.
blaze—an area of white that runs down the middle of the head from the forehead to the muzzle.
blocky—describes a head that is excessively square.
bloom—the glow or sheen on a coat in excellent condition.
blue—the correct coat color in the Bedlington or a dilute coat color that is incorrect in some other breeds.
blunt muzzle—a truncated or cut-off muzzle.
bobtail—a tail that is extremely short or non-existent as in the Old English Sheepdog.
body—the part of the dog that does not include the head and legs.
bolt—to flush game out of its lair.
bone—general term used to describe the size and shape of the legs. Bone is described as oval, round, or flat. Good bone means that the bones are substantial.
bossy shoulders—loaded or overly muscular shoulders.
bounce—term used to describe movement of the dog that is exaggerated in the up and down motion of the back.

bow hocks—hocks that are bowed out, synonymous with barrel hocks.
bowed front—forearms that bow slightly outward and then in again to the wrist.
brace—a pair of dogs of the same breed shown together.
brachycephalic—a skull that is wider than it is long.
break—(1) describes the stepdown from the skull to the muzzle. (2) the change in coat color from puppy coat to adult coat as in the Kerry Blue Terrier.
breeches—long hair on the rear legs sometimes called trousers or culottes as in the Schipperke.
breed—(1) the classification that distinguishes one type of dog from another. (2) show term used to designate the best dog of a particular kind.
brindle—a coat color that consists of a light ground color that is marked in a striped fashion by darker hairs as in the Boxer.
brisket—the sternum or the bottom of the rib cage. It is also called the keel.
broken coat—term used to describe Terrier coats that are a combination of harsh, wiry outer hair and dense, softer undercoat.
broken-up face—a foreshortened face with a pushed-in look as in the Bulldog.
brush—the tail.
bull neck—a somewhat short, thick, muscular neck.
burr—a crest or bump on the inside base of the rose ear.
butterfly nose—a nose that is spotted and not completely pigmented.
buttocks—the rump.
button ears—a semi-erect ear in which the top half folds forward.
camel back—a topline that has a gentle rise from mid-back to the end of the loin.
canine—the family of dogs and wolves.
canine teeth—the four large holding teeth.
canter—an easy gallop.
cap—color pattern on the head that resembles a cap as in the Siberian Husky.
capacious—large or roomy as in a capacious chest.
cape—a profuse mantle of long hair covering the shoulders as a cape might.

carpal joint—the wrist.
carpus—the bones of the wrist.
cat foot—a foot that is round like that of a cat.
character—the identifying quality of the dog and even the temperament of the dog.
chary—aloof in the presence of strangers
cheek—the area of the head below the eye that extends to the mouth.
cheeky—a head whose cheeks are too fleshy.
cherry nose—a flesh-colored nose.
chest—the thorax, which includes the area from the base of the neck to the diaphragm and contains the heart and lungs.
chin—the front and lower portion of the muzzle.
china eye—a blue eye that is flecked or spotted.
chiselling—the absence of excessive flesh as in chiselling under the eyes.
chops—the pendulous lower part of the upper lip or the flews.
cleft palate—a birth defect of the roof of the mouth in that the hard palate did not close completely.
clip—the trim or pattern of a clipped or scissored coat.
cloddy—heavy-set or too fleshy.
close coupled—the distance between the last rib and the thigh is short.
close-cupped foot—synonymous with cat foot as in the Great Pyrenees.
coarse—(1) describes a dog that is overdone and lacks subtle refinements. (2) It is also used to describe a harsh-textured coat.
coat—the combination of the outer hair and the undercoat of the dog.
cobby—a short bodied dog that is usually somewhat broad.
cocked ears—ears that are semi-erect.
collar—the color or coat pattern around the neck and shoulders.
collarette—a small mane or ruff around the shoulders.
compact—short in length as in compact body.
compact foot—synonymous with cat foot.
compact toes—synonymous with cat foot.
condition—the general physical status of the dog.
conformation—the overall structure of the dog that determines the breed qualities.

congenital—a birth defect that is not inherited.

corded coat—a coat in which the hair normally forms tight ringlets as in the Komondor and Puli.

corkscrew tail—a tail that spirals.

coupling—the area between the end of the rib cage and the beginning of the hindquarters.

cow hocked—the hocks are closer together than are the feet and point toward each other.

crabbing—a sidewinding gait usually resulting from over-angulation in the rear.

crest—the nape of the neck.

crook—(1) the inward turn of the forelegs on short-legged breeds as in the Basset Hound. (2) A twist at the end of the tail.

cropping—the cutting of ear leathers to make them smaller and to stand them erect as in the Miniature Schnauzer.

crossing—the action that results when the path of the two front or the two rear feet cross each other in forward movement.

crouch—a lowering of the hindquarters when the dog is standing resulting from weak muscles or excessive angulation.

croup—the area between the forward part of the hip joint and the buttocks which is over the pelvis.

crown—the top part of the skull.

cryptorchid—a male dog with neither testicle descended into the scrotum.

culotte—long hair that gives a trouser-like appearance to the rear legs as in the Schipperke.

cushion—lips that are thick as in the Shar-Pei.

cynology—the study of the dog.

dancing gait—a gait with mincing steps and a topline that bounces up and down.

dapple—a coat color in which the ground color is light and is mottled or spotted with a darker color or colors.

dead ears—a hanging ear that is immobile.

deadgrass—the straw-colored coat of the Chesapeake Bay Retriever.

deep-set eyes—eyes that are deeply seated in their sockets.

dentition—the tooth structure of the mouth.

dewclaw—the underdeveloped fifth toe.

dewlap—loose, hanging skin on the lower jaw and throat.

diaphragm—the membrane that separates the chest cavity from the abdominal cavity.

digit—the toe.

dish face—a muzzle that is concave between the stop and the nose.

dishing—synonymous with weaving.

disqualification—a fault in the dog that makes him ineligible to compete in bench show competition.

distal—farthest away from the core of the body.

dock—to shorten a tail by cutting off the end.

dolichocephalic—a long, narrow skull as in the Borzoi.

dome—the topskull.

domed skull—a rounded skull synonymous with apple skull or apple head.

dorsal—refers to the back.

double coat—a two-layered coat generally with coarse outer guard hairs and softer undercoat.

down face—a muzzle that drops between the stop and the nose.

down in pasterns—pasterns that are too sloping and weak.

drive—the rear propulsion of the dog.

drop ears—pendant or hanging ears.

dry neck—a neck free of excess flesh.

dudley—a nose that is not fully pigmented.

east-west feet—feet that do not point straight forward, but rather point slightly outward.

ectropion—a condition in which the lower eyelid is loose and forms a haw.

egg-shaped head—a head shaped like an egg as in the Bull Terrier.

elbow—the joint between humerus and the radius-ulna.

entropion—a condition in which the eyelid turns inward and causes the eyelashes to rub on the eye.

ewe neck—the nape of the neck is concave rather than convex.

expression—the appearance of the head which determines the breed character. It is a combination of the size, shape, and placement of the ears and the size, shape, and color of the eye, and the general combination of other head features.

face—the part of the head from the nose to the skull just behind the eyes.

fall—the long head coat.
fang—the canine or holding teeth.
feathering—long hair frequently found on the underside of the tail in some breeds.
feral—wild or undomesticated.
fibula—the narrower of the bones of the lower thigh.
fiddle front—describes the front legs of the dog. The elbows are wide apart, narrowing to the wrist and then flaring outward again.
fish-eye—a spotted or flecked eye.
flag—a long tail that is carried high.
flank—the area on the sides of the dog below the loin.
flare—a blaze that gets wider as it approaches the skull.
flared nostrils—nostrils that are wide open and not pinched.
flashing—white markings on the neck and face of the dog.
flat back—the topline of the back is flat and level, a fault in the Whippet.
flat bone—leg bone that is flat in shape rather than round or oval.
flat sided—the sides of the rib cage are flat rather than rounded.
flecks—small spots or spotting on the coat.
flews—the fleshy lower portion of the upper lips.
flex—the action of the closing of a joint.
fluffy—a dog that has an overabundant long, soft coat.
flyer—a novice dog that wins consistently.
flying ears—semi-hanging ears that are raised when the dog is at attention as in the Whippet.
forearm—the part of the foreleg that is formed by the radius and ulna and located between the elbow and the wrist.
foreface—the muzzle.
forequarters—consists of the shoulder, the upper arm, the forearm, the pastern, and the foot.
foxy—a fox-like appearance to the face as in the Cardigan Welsh Corgi.
freighting—the pulling work of a sledge dog.
frill—a ridge of hair running from the ear down the side of the neck to the chest.
fringe—long hair on the chest, belly, ears or tail.
front—the forequarters of the dog.

full eye—a protruding round eye.
furnishings—a more profuse coat on the ears, chin, tail, and legs.
furrow—a groove down the center of the skull.
gait—the movement of the dog.
gallop—a four-beat gait in which all feet are off the ground at one time.
gaskin—the lower thigh.
gay tail—a tail that is carried above the horizontal and sometimes over the back.
gazehound—a hound that hunts by sight.
girth—the circumference.
glass eye—a blue or speckled eye.
glaucous—a gray-blue color.
globular eyes—round, bulging eyes.
goggle eyes—eyes that protrude.
goose neck—a long, tube-like neck with little or no tapering.
goose rump—an excessively steep croup.
goose step—a gait in which the forelegs are lifted excessively high.
grizzle—a coat color formed by a mixture of black and white hair or black and red hair.
guard hair—the long, stiff hair of the outer coat.
hackles—guard hairs of the neck that lift when the dog is angry or excited.
hackney gait—action like a hackney pony. The front pastern and foot are lifted high and flexed in an exaggerated fashion. It is the typical gait of the Miniature Pinscher.
halo—darkly pigmented ring around the eye.
ham—the thigh.
hanging ear—an ear with no erectile tissue that hangs flat to the side of the head as in the Beagle.
hare foot—an elongated foot as in the rabbit.
harlequin—a coat color in which the ground color is white and is covered with patches of black or gray-blue as in the Great Dane.
haunch—the croup.
haw—the third eyelid.
head planes—the top surface of either the muzzle or the skull. Many breeds call for the head planes to be parallel to each other.

heel—the hock joint.
height—the measurement of a dog taken at the withers.
high stationed—a dog whose forelegs make up more than half of his height.
hindquarters—the rear portion of the dog composed of the pelvis, the femur, the tibia and fibula, the pastern and the foot.
hip—the joint between the femur and the pelvis. Some breed standards call for this joint to be 90 degrees.
hip dysplasia—a disease of the hip joint where the socket of the pelvis degenerates and no longer holds the head of the femur firmly.
hock—the ankle joint between the lower thigh and the rear pastern.
hollow back—a soft back whose topline dips.
hooded ears—ears whose edges curve forward as in the Basenji.
hook tail—a tail with a hook at the end as in the Briard.
horseshoe front—results when the elbows are set farther apart than the wrists.
hound lips—pendulous, square lips.
huckle bones—the forward tips of the pelvis prominent in the Afghan Hound.
ilium—one of the bones of the pelvis.
incisor teeth—the six small teeth between the canine teeth.
iris—the colored part of the eye that surrounds the pupil.
isabella—a light fawn color sometimes found in the Doberman Pinscher.
ischium—one of the bones of the pelvis.
jabot—the long hair on the chest between the front legs or lower part of the mane as in the Schipperke.
jacket—another name for the coat of the dog.
jowls—the soft pendulous lips as in the Bulldog.
keel—the lowest part of the chest, the sternum.
knuckled over—the wrist of the foreleg is bent forward.
knuckled-up toes—synonymous with cat foot.
Landseer—the black and white Newfoundland.
lank—lean or thin.
lateral—referring to the side of the dog.
layback—the angle that the shoulder blade makes from the vertical.
leather—the cartilagenous part of the outer ear.

leggy—a dog whose legs are longer than the norm.
length—the measurement of the dog from point of shoulders to the back of the buttocks.
level back—the dorsal spine is level.
level bite—has two meanings in the United States. (1) The upper and lower teeth meet edge to edge. (2) The teeth are of the same length. This is the meaning that is used in England.
ligament—a fibrous tissue that connects bones.
light eye—an eye that is light in color tending toward yellow.
linty—the texture of the coat of the Bedlington.
lippy—a mouth whose lips are too pendulous and loose.
liver—a reddish-brown color.
loaded shoulders—excessive development of muscles on the outer surface of the scapula.
loin—the area of the topline between the end of the rib cage and the beginning of the pelvis.
lolling tongue—a tongue that is too long and protrudes between the teeth when the mouth is closed.
loose elbow—the elbow is not held tightly to the side of the chest.
loose shoulder—a weak shoulder due to lack of proper musculature.
low stationed—a dog that is short in leg.
lower arm—the foreleg composed of the radius and ulna.
lower thigh—the part of the rear leg between the stifle joint and the hock joint composed of the tibia and fibula.
lozenge mark—a chestnut colored spot on the skull of the Cavalier King Charles Spaniel.
lumbar spine—the portion of spine over the loins between the thoracic spine and the sacrum.
lumber—an excessive amount of flesh.
luxated—dislocated as in the patella.
mandible—lower jaw.
mane—a long, abundant shawl around the neck and shoulders.
mantle—a cape-like blanket of dark hair over the shoulders and back.
markings—white spots or flashes on a darker-colored ground coat.
mask—dark shadings in a mask-like pattern on the head.
maxilla—the upper jaw.
median line—the groove running down the skull from the occiput to the stop.

merle—a coat with a lighter ground color covered with patches or spots of two-colored hair as in the blue-merle Shetland Sheepdog.

mesoticephalic—a skull that is of medium width.

metacarpus—the bones of the front pastern.

metatarsus—the bones of the rear pastern.

mincing gait—a gait characterized by short, choppy steps.

mismarked—a dog whose color pattern is incorrect.

molar—the large rear teeth, two on each upper jaw and three on each lower jaw.

molera—a soft spot in the center of the skull caused by incomplete closure of the parietal bones as in the Chihuahua.

monorchid—a male dog with only one descended testicle.

mottled—a two-colored coat that has a lighter ground color and darker blotches or spots.

mouth—often synonymous with bite and describes the manner in which the upper and lower teeth meet.

move close—describes the rear action of a dog when the hocks are excessively close to each other when the dog gaits.

movement—synonymous with gait.

multum in parvo—from the Latin meaning "a lot in a small space" and is used to describe the Pug.

Muschel—strongly developed burr of the ear as in the Saint Bernard.

muscle bound—excessive muscle development that interferes with movement.

musculation—the muscle development of the dog.

musculature—the arrangement of the muscles and their function.

muzzle—the foreface. That part of the head in front of the eyes.

muzzle band—a white band around the muzzle as in the Boston Terrier.

myofibril—a fibril found in the cytoplasm of muscle.

myofilament—one of the filaments of a myofibril.

nape—the back or top of the neck.

narrow front—a chest that is too narrow resulting in too little distance between the two front legs.

nasal septum—the fleshy division between the nostrils.

nuchal crest—top of the occiput.

obliquely set eyes—eyes whose outer corners are slightly raised.
occiput—the rearmost point of the skull. The occiput is prominent in some breeds and not in others.
occipital crest—the ridge that terminates at the occiput.
occlusion—the meeting of the teeth when the mouth is closed.
open class—a class in which any dog of a breed may be entered.
open coat—a sparse coat that lacks undercoat.
orange belton—an orange ticking pattern on the coat of the English Setter.
orb—the eyeball.
orbit—the eye socket.
otter tail—a well-furred tail, round and thick at the base and tapering to the tip as in the Labrador Retriever.
out at elbows—the elbows are not held close to the side of the rib cage.
outer coat—the outer, more harsh hair of a double-coated dog.
oval eye—the eye has an oval shape rather than a round shape.
oval feet—the feet are oval in shape rather than round and cat-like.
overfill—an area that is too fleshy. This is the opposite of chiselling.
overhang—an excessive brow above the eye as in the Pekingese.
overlay—a darker covering of hair over a lighter-colored section.
overreaching—because of an imbalance in angulation the rear legs reach beyond the paw print of the front feet. This usually results in crabbing.
overshot—the upper teeth extend too far forward and the incisors of the upper jaw do not touch the incisors of the lower jaw.
pace—a gait in which both legs of one side move forward at the same time.
pads—the soles of the feet.
padding—(1) A gaiting pattern in which the front foot is suspended slightly longer that it should be to avoid receiving the weight of the body before the forward thrust has been expended. (2) Additional thickness to the lips.
paddling—a gait that results from looseness of the elbows that causes the foot to kick out sideways.
palate—the upper inner surface of the mouth.

pants—breeches or longer coat on the rear legs.
paper foot—thin foot lacking in a well-developed pad.
pariah—a dog that was once domesticated but later returned to a wild state, an outcast.
parti-color—a two-colored coat with a ground color of white.
pastern—that part of the leg between the carpus and the foot of the foreleg or the tarsus and the foot of the hind leg.
patella—the kneecap.
paunchy—well rounded.
paw—foot.
peak—synonymous with occiput.
pelvis—the combination of fused bones that make up the pelvic girdle.
pencil markings—black lines on the top of the toes.
penciled coat—pily coat, crisp, a combination of harsh outer coat and soft undercoat.
pendant ears—ears that hang down close to the side of the head.
piebald—a white ground-colored coat with black patches.
pied—parti-colored.
pig eyes—eyes that are too small and set too close together.
pig jaw—a bite that is undershot.
pigeon breast—a dog lacking in forechest.
pigeon toed—feet that turn inwards.
pigmentation—the coloring of the skin.
pile—an undercoat that is thick and dense.
pily coat—penciled coat, crisp, or a combination of harsh outer coat and soft under coat
pincer bite—an even bite in which the lower edge of the upper incisors meets the upper edge of the lower incisors.
pinched-in front—excessively narrow front.
pinto—a white ground-colored coat with black patches.
pip—the tan spot above the eye in black and tan dogs.
pipe-stopper tail—a short, upright tail.
plane—the flat top surface of the skull or muzzle.
plumed tail—a tail that has long feathering at the end.
point of elbow—the topmost part of the forearm.
point of hock—the topmost part of the rear pastern.
point of shoulder—the joint between the scapula and the humerus.

points—spots of color on the black and tan dog.

pompon—the rounded tuft of hair on the hips and on the end of the tail as in the Poodle clip.

posting—a stance in which the front legs are extended too far forward and the rear legs are extended too far backward which resembles the stance of a rocking horse.

pounding—a jarring gait resulting when the front foot strikes the ground before the forward thrust of the dog has been expended. This is a very stressful gait.

premolars—the teeth between the canines and the molars. There are four on each side in both upper and lower jaws.

prick ears—ears that stand erect.

prosternum—the breastbone which projects forward past the point of shoulder.

proximal—refers to those parts which are close to the core of the body.

puffs—the bracelets on the lower legs of the Poodle.

quarters—the legs.

racy—a streamlined dog somewhat lacking in substance.

radius—one of the two bones of the forearm.

ram's nose—a muzzle that dips down to the nose, synonymous with aquiline nose.

rangy—a light-framed dog lacking in substance.

rattail—a tail which is not completely covered with hair towards the end.

reach—the forward extension of the front legs.

receding skull—the plane of the skull tilts backwards.

reverse scissors—a bite in which the front edge of the upper incisors is just behind and touching the inner edge of the lower incisors.

rib cage—the bone structure that surrounds the thoracic cavity.

rib spring—the outward and downward curve of the ribs.

ribbed-up—the back ribs extend backwards.

ridge—the pattern of opposite growing hair down the back of the Rhodesian Ridgeback.

ringtail—a long tail that has a curl or a ring at the end.

roached back—an unnatural rise over the back of the dog.

roan—a color resulting from the mixing of white and colored hair.

roll—the rotating side-to-side gait of breeds whose hindquarters are narrower than the forequarters as in the Bulldog.

roll a coat—a process in which the broken coat of a Terrier is continually worked or plucked so that it does not have to be completely stripped.

Roman nose—a muzzle that is convex between the nose and the stop.

root—the base of the tail.

rose ear—a drop ear that folds over and slightly sidewards to expose the burr.

round eyes—eyes that are circular in shape.

round foot—cat-like foot that is circular.

rounding—cutting or rounding the ears, as in the English Foxhound, to identify the pack to which it belongs.

ruff—a mane of off-standing hair around the neck and shoulders.

rump—the rear part of the dog that includes the croup and the buttocks.

runt—small in size.

sable—a coat that is fawn or golden whose hairs are black tipped.

saber tail—a tail with a slight curve that is carried upwards.

sacrum—the part of the spine that is behind the lumbar spine.

saddle—(1) The section of short hair down the back of the Afghan Hound. (2) The color blanket on the back of a dog.

saggital crest—the ridge running down the center of the skull.

sarcomere—one of the segments of the fibril of a striated muscle.

scapula—the shoulder blade.

Schwamm—a term for nose in the Saint Bernard standard.

scimitar tail—a well-curved tail, usually with feathering on the underside.

scissors bite—a bite in which the inner edge of the upper incisors meets the outer edge of the lower incisors.

scissura—median line between the eyes.

sclera—the white part of the eye.

scrambled teeth—teeth that are not in proper alignment.

scrotum—the sac that holds the testicles.

second thigh—the lower thigh or gaskin.

sedge—a color like dead grass.

self-colored—one colored.

semi-dropped ear—same as semi-pricked with the tip folded over.
semi-pricked ear—synonymous with semi-dropped ear.
set on—refers to the placement of ears or tail.
shank—synonymous with thigh.
shawl—synonymous with mane or ruff.
shelly—overly refined or lacking in substance.
shoulder—the scapula and the joint formed with the humerus.
shoulder blade—the scapula.
shoulder joint—the joint between the scapula and the humerus.
shuffle—a slow foot-dragging gait.
sickle hocked—the rear pastern is not perpendicular to the ground, but rather slopes forward so that the foot is not directly below the hock joint.
sickle tail—a semi-circular tail carried over the back.
sidewinding—in forward motion the longitudinal axis is not on the same line as the forward line of motion axis, synonymous with crabbing.
sinewy—free of excessive muscles or flesh.
single coat—a coat that has no undercoat.
single track—at speed both rear feet track on the same center line of forward motion as do both front feet.
skull—the bony structure that gives shape to the head.
slab sided—flat on the sides as either in the head or rib cage.
sloping back—a back that slopes from the withers to the loin.
sloping pastern—a pastern that is not perpendicular to the ground but rather slopes slightly forward.
sloping shoulders—the shoulders slant forward and downward from the withers to the point of shoulders.
smooth coat—a shorthaired coat.
snatch hock—a strongly flexed hock.
snipy—a finely pointed muzzle that is weak.
snow nose—a nose that fades in the winter months.
snowshoe foot—a compact, oval foot with well-arched toes and thick pads necessary for Northern breeds working in snow or ice.
soft back—a weak or hollow back.
soft mouth—a mouth that can carry a bird without doing damage to the bird.
soft palate—the soft fleshy appendage at the rear of the hard palate.

soundness—the physical condition of a dog that depends on a correct balance of bone and muscle.

speckling—a flecking of tiny colored spots throughout the coat as in the Australian Cattle Dog.

spectacles—colored circles of hair around the eyes that resemble eyeglasses as in the Keeshond.

spinal column—the backbone or vertebral column.

splash—irregular markings of white on a darker-colored ground.

splay foot—a foot that is flat with the toes well separated one from the other.

split nose—a nose that is divided on top as well as divided down the front, a disqualifying fault in the Great Dane.

split-up toes—toes well separated from each other.

spread—the distance between the forelegs.

spread toes—synonymous with split-up toes.

spring—synonymous with bounce.

spring of ribs—refers to the outward and downward curvature of the ribs as they branch off the spinal column.

square in body—a dog that is as long as he is tall.

square-set eyes—eyes set on a straight line drawn across the face.

squirrel tail—a long tail that is curved over the back.

stance—the pose or the position in which a dog stands.

stand-off coat—a coat whose outer hairs stand out separate from each other because of a dense undercoat.

staring coat—a coat that is dry and harsh and sometimes even curly at the tip of each hair.

station—refers to the height of the dog.

steep pasterns—pasterns that are upright or perpendicular to the ground.

steep shoulders—shoulders that are not well laid back and are more upright.

stern—the tail.

sternum—the breastbone.

stifle—the joint between the upper thigh and the lower thigh.

stilted gait—an up-and-down gaiting motion that results when a dog is poorly angulated.

stockhaarig—term used to describe the shorthaired coat of the Saint Bernard.

stop—the drop or depression between the planes of the skull and the muzzle.

straddle—a pose in which either or both the forelegs and the hindlegs are too wide apart.
straight front—when seen from the front, both legs are straight and parallel.
straight hock—a hock that has insufficient angulation.
straight in shoulders—the shoulders lack layback and are too upright.
straight in stifle—the stifle joint has too wide an angle.
subluxation—a condition in which a bone is dislocated as in the case of the patella.
substance—the amount of bone.
superciliary ridge—the bones of the skull that form the brow.
supra-orbital ridge—see superciliary ridge.
swan neck—synonymous to goose neck, a long thin neck that does not taper.
sway back—a back that sags or a hollow back.
swirl—the slight upward curve to the tail.
tarsus—the ankle.
team—a group of four dogs shown together.
tendon—the fibrous material that joins muscles to bones.
third eyelid—a membrane eyelid that is located at the inner corner of the eye.
thorax—the chest cavity.
throatiness—excess skin on the underside of the neck.
thumb marks—black spots on the lower leg just above the foot.
tibia—the broader of the two bones of the lower thigh.
ticked—spots of black or colored hair on a white ground.
tied-in elbows—elbows held in too closely to the side forcing the feet to turn outward.
tied-in shoulders—poor attachment of the shoulders resulting in a limited range of motion.
tight lips—lips that fit tightly to the structure of the jaw.
timber—synonymous with bone.
toe in—the feet point inwards rather than straight ahead.
toe out—the feet point outwards rather than straight ahead.
topcoat—the outer coat.
topknot—the tuft of long hair on the head.
topline—the upper outline of the dog from the withers to the croup.

topskull—the top of the head.
trace—the color line down the back of the fawn-colored Pug.
triangular eye—slightly more three-sided than the oval eye.
trichiasis—eyelashes growing in abnormal directions and causing damage to the eyeball.
tri-colored—a coat that has three colors in it.
trim—to clip or scissors the coat of a dog.
trot—the normal gait for the dog in the show ring. The right front leg and the left rear move forward at the same time followed by the left front leg and the right rear moving together at the same time.
trumpet—the temple of the dog.
tuck-up—the underline of the abdomen that raises from the end of the rib cage to the hindquarters.
tulip ear—an erect ear that is curved forward.
turn up—the upward curve of the muzzle from the stop to the nose.
two-angled head—a head whose planes are not parallel but are at an angle to each other.
type—the qualities that distinguish one breed from another.
ulna—the narrower of the two bones that form the forearm.
undercoat—the soft, short coat of hair that lies close to the body in dogs that carry a double coat.
underline—the opposite of topline. The line that traces the lower limits of the dog from the beginning of the sternum to the hindquarters.
undershot—describes a bite in which the lower teeth extend beyond the upper teeth.
unsound—a dog that cannot function normally because of defects in either his physical or mental condition.
upper arm—the humerus and surrounding tissue.
upper thigh—the femur and surrounding tissue.
upright pastern—a pastern that is perpendicular to the ground.
upright shoulders—shoulders with too little layback.
vent—the anus.
vertebra—one of the bones of the spinal column.
waist—the narrowing of the body behind the rib cage and over the loin area.
walk—a slow, four-beat gait.

wall eye—a flecked or spotted blue or white eye.
weaselness—a long, thin body resembling that of the weasel.
weaving—an incorrect gait in which the front feet or the rear feet or both cross over each other.
webbed feet—a foot with webbing between the toes seen in water dogs as an aid to swimming.
wedge-shaped head—a head that narrows gradually from back skull to front of muzzle.
weedy—describes a body that is underdeveloped without sufficient substance.
well-bent hock—a hock that is well angled.
well coupled—synonymous with short coupled with little distance between the last rib and the hindquarters.
well knit—body parts or segments closely and soundly joined.
well let down hock—indicates that the rear pastern is short.
wheaten—a coat of straw color.
wheel back—an exaggerated curve of the topline from the back through the croup.
whip tail—a stiff tail carried straight to the rear.
wide front—the front is wide when the distance between the two front legs is wider than normal.
wire coat—a broken coat with hard crisp hair in the outer coat.
withers—the area of the topline where the scapulae meet. It is the highest point of the back and is the spot where the height of the dog is determined.
work the coat—a method of rolling or plucking the broken coat of the Terrier on a continual basis to avoid completely stripping the coat
wrinkle—a loose fold of skin.
wrist—the joint between the forearm and the pastern.
wry mouth—a mouth in which the lower jaw is twisted and out of line with the upper jaws. The teeth do not meet correctly.